Angry at break

Angry at breakfast   Erik Jensen

ISBN 9781760644901

Published by Black Inc.
an imprint of Schwartz Books Pty Ltd
Wurundjeri Country
22–24 Northumberland Street
Collingwood VIC 3066, Australia
enquiries@blackincbooks.com
www.blackincbooks.com

9781760644901 (paperback)
9781743823439 (ebook)

 A catalogue record for this
book is available from the
National Library of Australia

Cover image: *Serious Problem* (2013) © Urs Fischer
Courtesy of the artist and Sadie Coles HQ, London
Photo: Mats Nordman

Cover and book design by Ziga Testen
with Kim Nastacha Mumm Hansen
Typesetting by Marilyn de Castro

For Mum and Dad, like everything
And Louisa, for everything else

Tony (2013–2015)

Malcolm (2015–2018)

Scott (2018–2022)

Anthony (2022–)

Compassion without anger can become merely sentiment or pity. Knowledge without anger can stagnate into mere cynicism and apathy.
—Jack Newfield

Frankly, despite my horror of the press, I'd love to rise from the grave every ten years or so and go buy a few newspapers.
—Luis Buñuel

Three-toed indifference

Until the age of five, I believed things only exploded and only rarely. The day I learnt this not to be true, I was trying to hold a papaya that I thought would be breakfast. As I lifted the fruit, its flesh ran out onto the table. Its juice had burnt into the timber and the air stung with its ripeness. That morning, I learnt the word "imploded".

I thought about this betrayal as I read over a decade of editorials from *The Saturday Paper*. I realise now that it is exceedingly uncommon for something to blow up. Much more likely, it will rot from inside. Australia is proof of that. Two of the past four prime ministers have been the worst in this country's history. The others have been better only by comparison. If there is something broken here, they broke it.

None of the problems in this book are insoluble. For each of them, the stumbles and repetitions reflect only the absence of wit among the politicians who lead us. Theirs is the grasping emptiness of power without imagination. They cannot see beyond themselves, can never bring their eyes to meet the horizon. Their world is shattered, irreparably, into fragments no greater than three years in length.

To read these pieces together is to read the story of our recent politics. It is a story of avarice and farce. The rhythms are of a country marching in place. The characters stay the same and do not develop character. Nothing happens and everything happens. Possibility is everywhere. A decade is lost. The great, sloth-eyed inertia of our politics, the three-toed indifference, conspires to make the country aimless and unchanging.

Sometimes, writing these pieces, anger would beat in my head like a drum. I found this confronting. I have always feared anger. To me it represents chaos and disorder. As a reporter, I was told it was forbidden. To express it was to lose objectivity. I realise there is a cunning purpose to this: anger is the engine of change and too much of the world does not want to change.

The first editorial in this collection was written six months before the paper launched. Through those months it existed as a kind of boundary stone, a marker of the paper's purpose, of the perimeter of its concerns.

Writing this introduction, I found an earlier draft and was immediately furious at myself for cutting the first paragraph: "A good newspaper is a compulsion. It runs the seemingly contradictory line of telling you today what you will need to know tomorrow and at the same time explaining last week. Reading it is an urge that must be satisfied before a day can properly begin."

The editorials that followed were almost all written in the half-hour before deadline. They were written in haste and anger. Often they were written to tell a story missed elsewhere. Sometimes they were there simply to underscore the paper's disgust, to scratch a jagged line below a news piece from several pages earlier.

That's what this book is: a jagged line between here and someplace else. Let's hope we get there soon.

Erik Jensen

Tony (2013–2015)

A young paper

Australia's first newspaper began in a shed behind Government House, published by a convict whose death sentence had been commuted to transportation for life. He was a shoplifter, later emancipated, and occasionally a poet. This is not a bad metaphor for the industry that followed.

Never have newspapers faced greater perils, both financially and from the more insidious creep of ideology. In this relief, it has never been clearer what they lack and what they most need: confidence, inquisitiveness, independence, occasional folly, passion, insight, moments of rage, frequent surprise. *The Saturday Paper* begins publication today because we are confident this is what we can offer.

We have no agenda and no single view. We owe nothing: to government, to vested interests, to a legacy at odds with the present and with itself. We are interested each week in only one objective: to drag news out of the narrows into which it has been forced and make a virtue of knowledge that is broad and deep, to try in a single paper the great task of explaining Australia.

Journalism has never lost its primacy – its place as society's most valuable fulcrum, the pivot between ordinary people and those who control them – but journalism has a way of talking itself into obsolescence. Complaint is the white noise of the newsroom. Despair is preferred over success. Failure is everywhere.

In place of this despair, we offer a bold faith in news. We offer politics in its stumbling comedy and messy truths. Policy as it fends off the ravages of compromise. Society as it struggles with change, pushing back and forth until it is given the space to understand what it is doing. Culture as it threatens collapse but somehow comes through instead with insight. We offer a newspaper that believes in Australia and what it can be.

The American columnist Jim Bishop produced one of the great descriptions of newspapers: "A newspaper is lumber made malleable. It is ink made into words and pictures. It is conceived, born, grows up and dies of old age in a day." This is the fleeting alchemy – the awing fact a newspaper ever makes it off the presses, let alone onto a front lawn – that gives print journalism its great magic. It is why we still believe in print: the miracle that will drive The Saturday Paper, the constant battle to deadline, the sense with each word and each unfolded lie that what we do is important and that it owes to its heritage the well-worn values of independence and objectivity.

And so here we are, this young paper with tenacious vision, a paper defiant of trends and conventional wisdom, trusting in a country that needs sophistication in place of sophistry, that yearns for calmer debate and better journalism. This is a newspaper for a country more serious than it is often credited with being. Its complexity will be hidden in its simple aspiration: to chronicle, unsparingly, the age in which we live.

Fundamentally, *The Saturday Paper* is about permission: permission for a country to look at itself unselfconsciously; for writers to tell stories that are ignored elsewhere, in ways that challenge orthodoxy; permission to question authority and provoke debate, to round up an issue, to yap and growl and demand we be better. We promise to be a small but handsome mongrel, a blue heeler cross of the press.

The forest from the trees

Nobody wants this. Environmentalists are against it. Unions don't support it. The Forest Industries Association has written to the prime minister, asking him to reconsider. But the Liberal Party is intent on ripping up the Tasmanian Forests Agreement. They want it undone and the amity it has brought gone.

The deal is part of an uneasy peace brokered last year, which allowed for an agreed amount of timber logging in exchange for the protection of key forest areas. After decades of rancour, it allowed timber workers and environmentalists to negotiate a compromise in Tasmania's forests. The agreement earmarked half a million hectares of forest for protection.

But after winning the Tasmanian election at the weekend, Liberal Premier Will Hodgman has said that reversing the deal is among his first priorities in government. Senator Eric Abetz had been banging this drum since well before the poll. The federal government had already begun the process of delisting 74,000 hectares of forest marked as having World Heritage value.

"We don't support, as a government and as a Coalition, further lock-ups of our forests. We just don't support it," Tony Abbott said at a dinner for timber workers this month.

"We have quite enough national parks. We have quite enough locked-up forests already. In fact, in an important respect, we have too much locked-up forest ... Getting that 74,000 hectares out of World Heritage listing, it's still going to leave half of Tasmania protected forever, but that will be an important sign to you, to Tasmanians, to the world, that we support the timber industry. When I look out tonight at an audience of people who work with timber, who work in forests, I don't see people who are environmental vandals. I see people who are the ultimate conservationists."

It was hard to know for whom this speech was delivered. It wasn't for the forestry workers thriving under the peace deal. Nor the union that supports it. Nor the industry association that wants to see it continue. It was as if Abbott was speaking to some part of Australia, far from Tasmania, that wants to know man might triumph over the trees.

This is a battle when the war has already been lost. Conservative government should be about steady government, but this is a government that thrives on chaos. Right back to his student days, Abbott has been a person who flourishes in commotion. On so many issues, the war mostly is over: the rights of women and gays, the science of climate change, the history of Aboriginal Australia, the protection of forests. But the stability of these settled scores does not suit a government more used to being an opposition than being in charge.

And so we have a forestry agreement ripped up, battles that have already reached their conclusions being dragged by skirmish back into life. Who this helps is not clear. Certainly, a battle from the past is a handy diversion from the future. There are old war horses who would like to fight again a war they have already lost.

This does not help Tasmania. It does not help the people who work in forestry, or in tourism. It is no help to a fragile economy with a pitiful record of unemployment.

Stoking instability is not the work of a conservative government, but in many respects this is not a conservative government.

Unsettled in Australia

In our streets, men are setting themselves ablaze. One is dead, another hopelessly burnt. On Christmas Island, women are reportedly attempting suicide in the hope their orphaned children might be given refuge. These people have fled one terrible regime, only to find another.

Tony Abbott calls this a "moral barrel". He will not be held over it. His empathy will not be extorted. "I don't believe any Australian would want us to capitulate to moral blackmail."

Perhaps not. Some, however, might expect compassion.

On sea, 153 Tamils are floating in the hold of a Customs vessel. They have been there for weeks and will be there for weeks more. It was only in the High Court – where a challenge was brought this week – that the government would confirm their existence. Until then, it had hedged and lied. Another 41 Tamils have already been handed back to the country they were fleeing.

That we have broken international law is not in question. The quibble is with our constitution, with the government's executive authority. Australia has the powers to turn back a boat, but not necessarily to ferry asylum seekers to the shores of other lands. Respected lawyers have asked whether this might equate to piracy. The United Nations has raised its concerns. Legal academics have warned that holding asylum seekers in this manner "amounts to incommunicado detention without judicial scrutiny". The shameful days of the *Tampa* have been invoked.

In Sri Lanka giving patrol boats to a regime accused of war crimes, the immigration minister did not waver. "The resolve of the Australian and Sri Lankan governments to stop people smuggling is stronger and greater than the people smugglers," Scott Morrison said this week. "To anyone here who may think of getting on a people smuggling voyage to Australia: don't believe the lies that the people smugglers tell you."

There is nothing new about this. Hawke gave it a go. Keating, too. Howard made an art of it – of the grim political calculus that says one can be endlessly cruel to those wretched souls who arrive here by boat and that the public will largely thank you for it. The polling is with them. Demonising asylum seekers wins elections. It persuades voters to blame queue jumpers for the things over which governments more correctly have responsibility, for being unable to find jobs or waiting too long in hospital lines. The language of this is fanciful – the queue – but the meanness is wholly simple.

It leaves our migration act nibbled at and patched up. Occasionally – indeed, with increasing frequency – the high court will peel off one of these Band-Aids. Yet governments don't stop. In Parliament House offices, amendments are readied. Elements of law are considered under the euphemistic title "exotic".

And the country, mostly, continues untroubled. Before these last awful events, polls returned saying most Australians thought we could be tougher on people seeking asylum by boat. As if the desert camps were not enough. As if the devil islands and caged children were not enough. As if the madness caused by temporary protection were a salve. As if these dark and damaged figures were here out of anything but desperation.

This is the logic that says refugees come both to take jobs and bludge welfare. It is the logic of moral barbarism. It is the logic of a polity that is coarse and hateful.

The boats have stopped. The cruelty has not.

Obama's call

The speech to the United Nations by US President Barack Obama this week was notable for its clarity on the issue of climate change and political responsibility. The basis of its candour is worth reproducing at some length, for those in this country who could benefit from similar frankness.

"Let me be honest," Obama said. "None of this is without controversy. In each of our countries, there will be interests that will be resistant to action. And in each country, there is a suspicion that if we act and other countries don't, that we will be at an economic disadvantage. But we have to lead …

"Yes, this is hard. But there should be no question that the United States of America is stepping up to the plate. We recognise our role in creating this problem. We embrace our responsibility to combat it. We will do our part. And we will help developing nations do theirs. But we can only succeed in combating climate change if we are joined in this effort by every nation, developed and developing alike. Nobody gets a pass."

Obama spoke as the man responsible for the world's largest economy and who leads a country that counts as its second-largest emitter. He was not without skin in the game.

For its part, Australia essentially boycotted the summit. Tony Abbott was purposefully absent from the session. Julie Bishop was there, but only to make the case for her party's farcical, unlegislated and disproved Direct Action plan.

Obama was clear in his agenda, however: climate change is the greatest problem facing the world, greater than terrorism or inequality or disease or any other threat. The science has been categorically decided. But the problem was being properly realised just as it was becoming too late to do something. Urgency was paramount. So was unity.

When Obama talks about interests resistant to action, he is talking to a hostile congress. He is talking to an element in the political class.

In Australia, however, we have an entire government bent on inaction. We have a government that won an election on the simple promise to destroy a tax broadly recognised as the best way to manage carbon emissions. This is a government so vociferous in its anti-science rhetoric that in opposition it saw public acceptance

of anthropogenic climate change go backwards only as the
literature proving its reality mounted.

Action on climate change in Australia, urgent as it is, will not
come from Abbott's government. This he has made clear a
thousand times since first deciding inaction would be the fissure
on which he would split the party room and win the opposition
leadership. It is a stubborn and unseeing position, blind to sense,
that will only be corrected by an informed and unyielding public.

Obama's UN speech, again: "Our citizens keep marching ...
We cannot pretend we do not hear them. We have to answer the
call ... We cannot condemn our children, and their children, to a
future that is beyond their capacity to repair."

Can and able

The immigration minister, Scott Morrison, got part way through his answer before he decided "appropriateness" was too strong a metric. It was too generous to the situation.

"Where appropriate, people ..." he said, halting himself, before restarting: "Where we're able to do so, people are returned to their country of origin. That's how the system works and that's how the system will continue to be applied."

Morrison was talking about the refoulement of Zainullah Naseri, the first Hazara to be sent back to Afghanistan after Australia rejected his claim for refugee status. As reported in The Saturday Paper last week, he was in the country only three weeks before he was kidnapped and tortured by the Taliban.

Naseri, who told his story in the course of several long interviews with the journalist Abdul Karim Hekmat, and whose account is supported by video footage taken by Afghan police, was deported after the Refugee Review Tribunal ruled there was "not a real risk the applicant will suffer significant harm".

Shortly before Naseri was deported, an Afghan-Australian, Sayed Habib Musawi, was tortured and killed by the Taliban on the same route where Naseri was kidnapped. The tribunal found, however, "there is a route from Kabul to Jaghori that is secure". This is the difference, one presumes, between "appropriate" and "able".

Morrison has indicated that in the wake of *The Saturday Paper*'s report he asked his department to launch "appropriate inquiries" into Naseri's case. "I'll see where that course takes us," he said. He has done nothing to halt the deportation of seven more Hazaras whose applications have been rejected. They will be sent to the same troubled country and the risk of a similar fate.

"I should stress this: people who are found not to be refugees in Australia have been through a very long, some would argue too long, process to determine whether Australia has an owed obligation of protection to that person," Morrison said.

"People who are returned in these circumstances are found not to be refugees and not owed a protection by the Australian government. And on that basis they have no lawful basis for remaining in Australia."

On this point, Morrison is emphatic. He will not be moved by torture or death. If it can be done, it will be done. The measure, we now understand, is this: Where we are able to do so.

"Life is too bitter," Naseri told Afghan police after they found him, beaten and weary, a chain attached to his ankle where the Taliban had restrained him. "It would have been better if they killed me."

Morrison's promise that "inquiries" are being made is insufficient. As minister, he has a pathetic record on transparency. Should any inquiries be conducted, we can have no confidence in their findings being revealed.

At the very least, the seven people Australia intends to send back to Afghanistan must be allowed to stay until the safety of the country can be ascertained. The Refugee Review Tribunal must be open about the information that led to its decisions.

The issue is larger than that, however, and the response needs to be larger. It cannot be left with the minister or his department. As reports of sexual abuse spill from the detention centre on Nauru, and Manus Island looks increasingly like a failed endeavour, the case for a royal commission into our treatment of asylum seekers becomes stronger by the day.

Unfair maiden

It is instructive, periodically, to go back and read the maiden speeches of government ministers. They are the stuff of aspiration, benchmarks of morality set before the realities of Canberra and of cabinet have worn them away.

Scott Morrison gave his maiden speech on Valentine's Day 2008. It was six minutes to midday when he intoned on "the values and vision that I intend to bring to this House".

In among the platitudes and paeans to free markets and Christianity, the quotes from Jeremiah and Desmond Tutu and Bono, he spoke of an Australia that was "above all, generous in spirit", that would "share our good fortune with others, both at home and overseas, out of compassion and a desire for justice".

He spoke of responsibilities: "As global citizens, we must also recognise that our freedom will always be diminished by the denial of those same freedoms elsewhere, whether in Australia or overseas."

He spoke of the need to increase foreign aid, which his government has since cut, of "values of loving kindness, justice and righteousness", of "compassion", of his commitment "to respect the rule of law".

It is worth considering these hopes as Morrison shepherds through the parliament a knot of bills that would undermine the rule of law and strip what little compassion is left from this country's bastard system of processing asylum seekers.

This sentiment is worth recalling, too: "Family is the stuff of life and there is nothing more precious." And so is this: "It is my hope that all Australians could have the same caring and supportive environment that was provided to me by my parents."

One of Morrison's bills would prevent children who were born in Australia to asylum seekers from gaining citizenship. It would also shield the government from claims over human rights breaches. Among the suite of bills is capacity for Morrison to revoke citizenship on the basis of character, without the support of a court.

The Morrison who once spoke of "global citizens" wants to reinterpret Australia's obligations to the UN refugee convention and legislate for the forcible turn-back of boats and people regardless of international law. Rights to appeal decisions will also be stripped.

What is perhaps most extraordinary in these changes, however, are the powers they confer on Morrison. He alone will have the ultimate say in cases. The logic is bizarre: "As an elected Member of Parliament, the Minister represents the Australian community and has a particular insight into Australian community standards and values and what is in Australia's public interest. As such, it is not appropriate for an unelected administrative tribunal to review such a personal decision of a Minister on the basis of merit, when that decision is made in the public interest."

There are those who see this as a power grab – a means of proving himself through expanded responsibility, in anticipation of a cabinet reshuffle. But it is about more than that. This is about the stubbornness of a government whose overreach on asylum seekers is too frequently frustrated by the courts and who want now to legislate a way around those courts. Taken together, these bills are an appalling assault on due process and the Australia Morrison so optimistically described six years ago. One hopes he also reads his maiden speech periodically.

Costs benefit paralysis

The attacks on journalism in this country are many and insidious. Laws criminalise reporters and their sources. Government monitoring is an unhappy and constant reality. National security is used as a cover for restricting scrutiny or removing it entirely.

None of this should be ignored or lightly accepted. But in broader terms, the greatest threats to journalism in this country are vindictive and ill-balanced defamation laws. The threat is greater because it is pervasive and its effects deadening to all debate.

The conclusion of Joe Hockey's defamation action against Fairfax this week was a case in point. He lost on all key imputations, and yet the proceedings may still cost Fairfax somewhere in the order of $1.3 million. The cost of defending the case was five times more than the damages Hockey actually won.

The extraordinary price of both bringing and defending defamation actions make the laws largely about defending privilege. It is no coincidence that the richest Australians are also the most litigious.

Defamation stands to make journalist and publishers timid. For some, this is the residual benefit of these actions. No flaw was found in the reporting of Hockey's involvement with paid access at the North Sydney Forum. Damages were calculated on an errant poster and a few stray tweets. But for journalists reporting on the powerful, and for the organisations publishing this reportage, the impact of a case such as this is numbing.

For small media organisations, even winning a defamation case can imperil an operation. *New Matilda* makes this explicit. Its latest subscription drive is "to try and cover some of our burgeoning legal costs".

Tens of thousand of dollars can be spent exchanging letters before a complaint gets to court, if ever. The risks produce settlements and apologies that can be more about avoiding costly legal action rather than about what is right and correct. The Hockey decision will only cement this.

In celebrating his win, pyrrhic as it was, Hockey said: "After nearly 20 years in public life I took this action to stand up to malicious people intent on vilifying Australians who choose to serve in public office to make their country a better place. Whilst the cost of this action has been considerable for me, my family and friends, it has been far greater for Fairfax Media."

The latter part of this is true. The first part is nonsense. Hockey's reputation is in no way repaired by the court because the court found it had been fairly damaged. The story was accurate. It was written not by malicious people bent on vilifying public officials but by journalists doing their job. Public life would be better if there were more of this, not less.

Australia desperately needs its defamation laws reformed, as has happened in Britain and Canada. Truth, while an absolute and useful defence, should be allowed to be proved in a tribunal without the wild costs of a court. Discussions should be between principals, not lawyers. If imputations are accepted, they should then be tested at a higher level and with representation.

This is not to defend the publication of reckless misinformation. It is to protect against the vexatious use of a system that has grown to favour the rich and powerful.

Even in celebrating, Hockey will be several hundred thousand dollars worse off for this case. If that alone is not proof the system is broken, it is hard to think what might be.

Reputation is expensive. Especially when you are buying it.

Going to war

As you read this, Australian bombs are probably already falling on Syria. Fighter jets are likely flying sorties. Where a month ago the foreign minister, Julie Bishop, said it was too uncertain to drop humanitarian aid over Syria, lest it become a "terrorists' picnic", now Australian air strikes will rain.

"It is quite clearly in Australia's national interest," the defence minister, Kevin Andrews, said, "because, as we know, Daesh continues to provide a security threat, not just to Iraq and those regions of Syria in the Middle East, but it reaches out here to Australia."

This mission is conducted with the support of Labor, but not with a debate in the parliament. Legally, one is not required. Sufficient power is invested in cabinet to give the approval. But there is no strong argument for forcing this decision without first making its case on the floor of the parliament.

Secrecy is not an argument. The government's intentions were flagged weeks ago, when Tony Abbott insisted he had been called on by the United States to offer assistance – despite numerous reports suggesting the inverse had happened.

Urgency, too, is a fallacious reason. Nothing is being decided that a proper parliamentary debate would unduly slow. As it is, no one is suggesting Australia's contribution will be a pace-changer in the conflict.

None of this is an argument against Australia's further involvement. The case is strong on many fronts, the need in this mission to protect Iraq's nascent democracy just one aspect.

But a lack of debate means this case has not been made. Kevin Andrews' assertion that Daesh's threat extends to Australia is evidence of the hollow arguments standing in for proper discussion.

It seems that nothing has been learnt from John Howard's commitment of Australian forces to the Second Gulf War, a conflict most accept was poorly argued and more poorly executed, the repercussions of which Abbott's air strikes will partly attempt to remedy. "I felt embarrassed, I did," Howard said last year, regarding the faulty intelligence on which he went to war without parliamentary debate. "I couldn't believe it, because I had genuinely believed it."

At the time, Tony Windsor was critical of the decision and the refusal to debate it. He is again. Writing in *The Saturday Paper* last year, as Australia became involved in Iraq, he made the following point: "There is something wrong when an elected government refuses to debate in its own parliament the decision to go to war, when one of the main reasons for intervention is to help countries in violent conflict to establish the right to debate and make their own decisions."

It is too late now to hope that Abbott's decision will be debated in parliament. As he continues to look for distractions with which to buttress his leadership, it is troubling to consider why it was not.

Kicking the Abbott

It is no exaggeration to say Tony Abbott is the worst prime minister Australia has had. To the extent that his brief and destructive leadership of the country is remembered, it will not be remembered well.

Abbott is a prime minister without a legacy. In attempting to defend one this week, he came up with not much: some jobs, a few trade agreements, an infrastructure project, a border protection regime founded on human rights abuses, a royal commission so compromised by bias its own commissioner had to consider removing himself.

Abbott governed for the past and the few conservatives desperate to continue living there. He governed against science and in contempt of the environment. He governed in opposition to social equality, in terror of reform. His was a government of fear and avoidance, a rolling sideshow anxiously avoiding the fact it had nothing to add and no idea what to do.

Abbott spent his time in opposition degrading the office of the prime minister. His was a campaign of debasement: a coarsening of debate, a running down of the respect once stored in the institution. Those who say he was a fine opposition leader do so in error. There is no victory in destroying what you set out to win.

On prevailing at the 2013 election, he placed on his head a small and tinny crown. He did nothing to repair it in the years that have passed since. Indeed, he only added to its dents and tarnish.

He treated law like a plaything. He made policy at odds with the country's own constitution. He fought consensus and held out against change. He refused humility. He let run the island camps where women and children are raped and men killed. He turned in from the world. He mocked treaties. He failed obligations. He fed prejudice wherever he could.

He was a coward with reform. He left the tax system lumbering and unfair. He failed to articulate policy. He hectored the ABC, cowing it and becoming ludicrously involved in editorial processes. He shunned innovation. He craved distraction.

Abbott's great fear, and the fear of those people left supporting him, is tomorrow. He is fearful of same-sex marriage. Fearful of an economy remade by climate change. Fearful of the fair distribution of taxes. Fearful of power as it ebbs away from the places where it was once concentrated. But tomorrow is always close; his prime ministership was always doomed.

Abbott is an experiment that failed. He is proof that Australia cannot be governed from the far right, just as it cannot be governed from the far left. He was the last hope and final holdout of a group of people wishing desperately against a modern Australia.

His time in the office leaves a hole in this country's agenda, a period of incompetent stasis, two wasted years we must now get back.

He will not be missed. He should not be praised. He was a failure selfishly wishing that the world would fail with him. We can only hope his like will not be seen again.

Malcolm (2015–2018)

Dutton for punishment

There is a simple reason Peter Dutton is still in cabinet. It is
not for his competence or his famous rapport with the department.
It is certainly not for his intelligence.

Peter Dutton remains in cabinet as a reminder that Malcolm
Turnbull will not be swayed by compassion on the issue of asylum
seekers. He will not attempt to clear Manus or Nauru, despite the
terrible abuses that take place there.

Dutton remains immigration minister to give succour to
those in the party room worried that the bad old days might be
over, that asylum seekers might be treated with dignity and the
useful toxicity might be bled from the refugee debate.

This week, Turnbull went so far as to say he was "concerned"
by conditions in offshore detention camps. An ordinary person
might be more than "concerned" by state-sponsored internment
camps that have been condemned by the United Nations and the
country's own Human Rights Commission, that violate accords
on torture and are notable for the deaths of men and the rape and
mistreatment of women and children.

Yet "concerned" is still too much for the Liberal Party.
Immediately Malcolm Turnbull was stressing that this concern
would not metastasise into decency.

"There will be no resettlement of the people on Manus and
Nauru in Australia. They will never come to Australia," he said.
"Now, I know that's tough, we do have a tough border protection
policy, you could say it's a harsh policy, but it has worked."

Any changes to policy, he stressed, would involve cabinet and
be conducted in a "considered way". The camps where children
attempt suicide were "not an ideal environment". But there would
be no "backward step". Turnbull's government was
"doing everything we can to encourage them to return to where
they came".

Dutton was there behind him: "The PM has made it very
clear that people who try to come to our country illegally by boat
will never be settled here."

It was not enough for Andrew Bolt, and those like him.
"Malcolm Turnbull has made his first mistake in playing
the uncomfortable role of a conservative," he wrote, "giving the
impression he will soften our border laws."

And again: "Malcolm Turnbull on Sky News this morning sent a dangerous signal. He refused to rule out changes to our border policies, and thanked a journalist for caring about illegal immigrants on Manus Island and Nauru. Uh-oh."

There is no margin for concern in the minds of conservatives. Not that Turnbull has shown much compassion in this area. He was happy to use the boats to his advantage as opposition leader.

But immigration and the environment are the two areas in which he will be most watched by those on his side of politics who wish he was on someone else's.

It is why, in remaking his cabinet, he did not remake these portfolios. While Greg Hunt may yet develop, Dutton will not. He is without ideas or subtlety. As long as he remains he will be hopeless and so will be the few thousand souls trapped in offshore detention.

This is one of the shameful truths of politics that even a new leader with staggering public approval cannot fix.

Meta commentary

As Monday tripped into Tuesday this week, Australia wandered blindly into an age of mass surveillance. Under the Telecommunications (Interception and Access) Amendment (Data Retention) Act 2015, a record of all communications and internet activity will be kept for a mandatory period of two years, to be accessed without warrant by a select group of agencies.

The act is as lumpy as its title, and the implementation lumpier still. But the heart of it is not terribly complicated. Edward Snowden, the whistleblower behind the revelation of mass surveillance by the US National Security Agency, put it this way: "Beginning today, if you are Australian, everything you do online is being tracked, stored, and retained for two years."

On Twitter, Snowden posed a question. His answer was more persuasive than any argument yet made for the legislation that was clumsily introduced to the parliament last year and sluggardly debated by both sides of the house. "Ask yourself: at every point in history, who suffers the most from unjustified surveillance?" Snowden wrote. "It is not the privileged, but the vulnerable. Surveillance is not about safety, it's about power. It's about control."

When Labor attorney-general Nicola Roxon proposed an almost identical scheme in 2012, Malcolm Turnbull said it seemed "to be heading in precisely the wrong direction". It was, and it remains that way.

The attorney-general's department maintains that there is no need for warrants in accessing metadata. It falsely claims that it is not kicking down doors. "Warrants are typically reserved for the most intrusive powers, such as the power to use force to enter a home, to intercept phone calls, or to arrest a person. Many powers, including access to metadata, simply do not rise to that level."

But the effect on society of laws that pretend to be tackling serious crime but could easily be used to target whistleblowers or activists is chilling. It is not enough to say the government would not do this, as ministers have argued: they already are. The thuggish hunt for the sources of stories revealing conditions in offshore detention camps is but one example.

"Metadata is the basic building block in nearly every counterterrorism, counterespionage and organised and major crime investigation," a spokeswoman for the attorney-general told Fairfax this week. "It is also essential for child abuse and child pornography offences that are frequently carried out online."

All this is true. None of it explains why the legislation allows agencies to act without warrants, to remove the courts as a buffer to check excess and protect the rights of citizens.

In March, Turnbull gave a bizarre interview to David Speers, which remains his most sensible commentary on the legislation to date. He made a quick list of services that can circumvent the act: Skype, Viber, WhatsApp, Wickr, Threema, Signal, Telegrammer, FaceTime. "There's a gazillion of them."

Having offered a grocery list, he explained the function: "All that the telco can see, insofar as it can see anything, is that my device has had a connection with the Skype server or the WhatsApp server; it doesn't see anything happening with you. There are always ways for people to get around things, but of course a lot of people don't, and that's why I've always said the data retention laws, the use of metadata, is not a silver bullet. It's not a 100 per cent guarantee. It is one tool in many tools."

There are many good reasons for retaining metadata, and for using it in law enforcement, but there are no good reasons for taking the courts out of this process. Turnbull is right about one thing: there are ways around the legislation. Until we can be satisfied that the information is not being misused to target whistleblowers and curtail freedoms, these alternative services should be favoured.

The public failed to effectively oppose these laws before they were passed. It is now the public's responsibility to see that they at least skirt them. Complacency is too dangerous an option.

Deathly silence

This week, Philip Nitschke agreed to stop giving advice on
assisted dying. As part of an arduous list of terms set out by the
Medical Board of Australia, he will not discuss any form of
voluntary euthanasia with patients, even after they have initiate
such a conversation. He will not address workshops on assisted
dying, or practise medicine outside the Northern Territory. He
will no longer engage in any of the advocacy work for which he is
known. His name will be removed from the book he co-authored,
The Peaceful Pill Handbook.

In exchange, the Medical Board of Australia will halt
proceedings for a tribunal hearing into Nitschke's professional
conduct. He says he does not have the million dollars that would
have been necessary to defend it. He had already spent $250,000
in the NT Supreme Court to prove the board's suspension of
his registration last year had been unlawful. Having been silenced
after decades of advocacy, he apparently intends to focus
on refining a comedy show he took to the Edinburgh Fringe in
August. This could be a joke, if it were funny.

"The role of the Medical Board of Australia is to protect
the public and manage risk to patients ..." the MBA said in
a statement. "The Board will be making no further comment on
this issue."

This is not a medical issue. It is a free speech issue. Patients
are not to be protected from prescriptions in these orders; they are
to be protected from ideas. Great length and expense have been
gone to in defence of the status quo.

In Melbourne this week, the day after the board made public
its tawdry deal, Andrew Denton delivered the Di Gribble
Argument. His subject was the case for voluntary assisted dying.
It is an argument with which the majority of Australians agree,
but it was put with a force of eloquence that reminded why this
issue must be discussed – even if the Medical Board, and the
Australian Medical Association, and the various palliative care
bodies, would rather it was not.

It must be discussed because until we have laws in place
that allow doctors to support patients who choose to die we will
have a system of care that is forced to live in the shadows, that
criminalises compassion and enshrines suffering.

Denton's research had taken him through systems in Oregon and the Netherlands and elsewhere. Nowhere did he find laws abused. If anything, officials were surprised by how infrequently they were used. In the end, people do not want to die.

But they should have the right to die, and a regulatory system that makes safe that right. The alternatives are imprecise and brutal: prolonged opiate deaths, with and without pain, or lonely and makeshift suicides.

And yet, because we do not talk about this, politicians are unmoved by overwhelming support for it. The elderly continue to improvise their deaths, their agony preferred to the shred of leadership necessary to change this system.

Nitschke's forced silence is the silence of political cowardice. It is a cowardice that will not lift until the public asks loudly for its end.

State of redress

George Brandis is yet to respond to the letter on his desk. What it requests is not terribly complicated. The Royal Commission into Institutional Responses to Child Sexual Abuse says it needs an answer by Christmas. State attorneys-general would like one sooner.

The letter asks Brandis for his position on a national redress scheme for victims of child abuse, the royal commission's key recommendation.

The elements of the scheme are simple: a direct and personal response from the institution where the abuse occurred, which includes detail of how future abuse will be prevented; access to appropriate psychological care; and a monetary payment that attempts to recognise the suffering of the abused.

The scheme would be largely funded by the states and institutions such as the Catholic Church, but it requires a federal framework. This is in part because of the unsatisfactory way current schemes have been run. There are too many roadblocks. Too much confusion. "In our view," a statement from the commission reads, "the current civil litigation systems and past and current redress processes have not provided justice for many survivors."

New South Wales and Victoria already support the redress scheme. They are committed to bringing other states and territories on board. The federal opposition also supports the scheme, although it has committed only $33 million in funding.

But the government itself has been silent. Without it, the key recommendation of the royal commission cannot be acted on.

What is at stake is extraordinary, the depth of suffering extreme. This royal commission has made more referrals for police investigation than any other in the country's history. Already, 792 cases have been directed to authorities. There are more than police can process. Some 240 investigations are running and 23 prosecutions are under way.

The commission has conducted more than 4200 private interviews with people who have been abused. Another 1400 are waiting to testify. Each week, that list grows by about 40.

Behind these numbers are terrible stories. They are stories of innocence betrayed and institutions that met these victims with unfeeling cruelty; institutions that conspired to help paedophiles and disregarded children, that prolonged for decades the abuse they knew was happening.

A scheme for the redress of this suffering can never be wholly sufficient. The trauma is too large, too various. But it offers a very basic level of understanding how a victim of child abuse might navigate a system of complaint and civil recourse.

It is expensive, but much of that cost will be to private institutions where abuse occurred. Beyond managing the scheme, the input from the federal government would be minimal.

Having seen the previous government's courage in establishing the royal commission, the least this government could do is endorse its recommendations. The least George Brandis could do is respond to the letter on his desk.

Christmas messaging

The pictures released by Peter Dutton's office show broken glass and charred walls. Two men appear to brandish a flare. Drone footage shows buildings well alight.

These are the first images out of the Christmas Island detention centre in years, and The Saturday Paper has decided not to publish them. The reason is simple: they are propaganda.

For the most part, it is relentlessly difficult to get information from the minister on offshore detention. Questions are ignored or answered in a bureaucratic patois devoid of fact. Access is impossible. Secrecy is the cancer of this system.

But on the question of rioting on Christmas Island this week, Dutton was everywhere.

He spoke to Paul Murray: "In terms of Christmas Island – because I do think that people conjure up this view about boat people when they think of Christmas Island detention centre – it's not that anymore."

To Ray Hadley: "If they're on visas and they fail the character test then we've cancelled their visa on that basis. So we're talking about some pretty serious characters here."

To ABC News Radio: "The government has been very clear about the fact that we have a hardened population within Christmas Island immigration detention centre."

To Sky News: "Officers obviously make professional judgements about the individual cases and they will look at whether or not, for example, somebody off a boat has sexually assaulted somebody out in the community. And that person would be treated then the same as anybody else who may have committed that sexual assault or grievous bodily harm, or whatever the nature of the crime may have been."

Dutton's purpose is not difficult to ascertain. He wants to persuade the public that the people on Christmas Island are child abusers and bikies, that they are hardened criminals. He told Hadley 113 people in the centre had been charged with "serious criminal offences". But that leaves 86 who had not been. They are the people Dutton does not talk about.

Fazel Chegeni was not among this number. He was already dead.

Chegeni was on Christmas Island at the minister's discretion. There was no question about whether Chegeni was a refugee. He had been tortured in the country of his birth, a member of Iran's Kurdish minority. His body was scarred with these facts.

Chegeni was deemed unfit for community release after a one-minute argument in the mess of Curtin detention centre, which led to an assault charge and a good-behaviour bond.

No court found him a risk to the community. But in the four years since he arrived by boat seeking asylum, he had been free only six months.

After the death of his sister, he had twice threatened suicide. Instead of being offered help, he was pushed further into the byzantine architecture of our detention system, from Brisbane to Darwin and finally to Christmas Island.

Chegeni's death ignited the rioting on Christmas Island, which caused what Dutton says is $10 million worth of damage. Yet we have not been told what caused Chegeni's death. Dutton has not said, and in only a few interviews was he actually asked.

Much easier to talk about law and order, to demonise a population on a distant island, far from the scrutiny of the press. Much easier to release pictures of burnt-out rooms than to talk about the innocent people held in them.

Once the federal police regained control of the centre, one of their first actions was to confiscate mobile phones. The brief flow of information again stopped.

"Our job," Dutton said this week, "is to make sure that people that have had their visas cancelled because of character failures or where they've committed serious criminal offences – they've had their visas cancelled and they're held in detention – our responsibility is to return them to their country of origin as quickly as possible."

The death of Ms Dhu

They laughed as she died, the inquest heard. They said she was lying, that she was carrying on "like a two-year-old child".

Ms Dhu was in police custody when she breathed for the last time. Her partner, Dion Ruffin, was in the cell beside hers. He heard her moaning, chocking on vomit, struggling to breathe. It went on for three days.

Ruffin said that in her last moments in the cell he heard a thump of some kind. Then nothing. "I heard this loud bang and [her] cry for help ended."

Ms Dhu was 22. She was held at Western Australia's South Hedland police station because she had failed to pay fines. She was Aboriginal.

Closed-circuit television footage played at the inquest into her death this week showed police attempting to lift her from the bed in her cell. She falls back, lifeless. A female officer holds open the door of Ms Dhu's cell while another officer drags her from the room by her hands, her body trailing on the floor.

The inquest heard police thought Ms Dhu "was faking it". She pleaded to go to hospital, showed her bluish hands, but police "felt the transfer was not urgent". The shift supervisor noted Ms Dhu "appears to be suffering withdrawals from drug use and is not coping well with being in custody".

Police carried Ms Dhu "like a dead kangaroo" to the back of a LandCruiser. They held her by her arms and legs, her body hanging between them in a slack arc. No one sat beside her. No one comforted her. She moaned again as the car's door slammed. A tape records the voice of a male officer: "Oh, shut up."

Ms Dhu's father has already testified at the inquest. His pain is raw. "They shouldn't have treated anyone like that. They left her there like a dog, to die."

Ms Dhu died of pneumonia, septicaemia and complications from a rib fracture. A simple X-ray would have diagnosed this. She was never given one.

Ms Dhu should not have died. She should never have been locked up for failing to pay fines. She should never have had her cries ignored, her health so overlooked. She should never have been mistrusted, mocked, forgotten.

Two decades have passed since the Royal Commission into Aboriginal Deaths in Custody. Still not enough has changed. Still its recommendations have not been implemented in full.

The incarceration of Indigenous people remains wildly disproportionate. Indigenous people are still locked up on trivial matters, dealt with by a legal system that would never treat a white Australian the same way. They are hounded with paperless arrests and inconsequential charges, fed into a machine that has no care for them, that is witless in its punishment.

The numbers are obscene, but they are bloodless. For two decades the system has been unmoved by them. The status quo becomes an excuse.

Much is known and much doesn't change. Ms Dhu died without dignity or reason. She died because a system didn't care enough to make sure she would live.

She was 22. She was Aboriginal. She had not paid her fines. These were her only crimes.

False gods

It is important, occasionally, to remember that the Australian Christian Lobby is nothing like it sounds.

Certainly, it is a lobby. The group, a registered private company, commands meetings with leaders of both major parties. It describes itself as "a credible Christian voice in the corridors of power" and boasts of "strong relationships with politicians and policymakers".

But to say that this lobby represents "Australian Christians" is a hopeless stretch. When the Australian Christian Lobby speaks, it speaks for an acetous few: a couple of Pentecostals and a few loon Baptists. Theirs is a false authority. Their influence belies their number.

Their chair is Jim Wallace, AM, a former SAS commander who says things such as, "I certainly believe that homosexuality is a sin – you know, I think that's an orthodox Christian view." He calls abortion "a slice of Western culture which only reinforces notions of the cheapness of life".

He says: "I think we're going to owe smokers a big apology when the homosexual community's own statistics for its health – which it presents when it wants more money for health – are that it has higher rates of drug-taking, of suicide, it has the life of a male reduced by up to 20 years ... we need to be aware that the homosexual lifestyle carries these problems and ... normalising the lifestyle by the attribution of marriage, for instance, has to be considered in what it does encouraging people into it."

Their managing director is Lyle Shelton. He was once a journalist and came to the lobby after a failed tilt at the Queensland parliament. He says things such as: "The prime minister who rightly gave an apology to the Stolen Generation has sadly not thought through the fact that his new position on redefining marriage will create another."

This week, Shelton argued that anti-discrimination legislation should be suspended in the lead-up to any plebiscite on same-sex marriage, so that the "no" campaign might be freely put.

He said: "I think the threshold for offence under many of these state-based anti-discrimination laws is way too low."

He said: "We're concerned about people being taken to human rights commissions around Australia simply for advocating marriage between a man and a woman and right to the child to, wherever possible, be allowed to be loved and raised by their mother and father."

This is an outrageous nonsense. If Shelton's arguments depend on vilification, they are scarcely arguments. They are bigotry. They are hate.

But it is worse than that. Shelton's argument for an override to anti-discrimination laws only highlights the concessions for religious groups already won in these laws. It is because of groups such as his that a church can lawfully sack gay men from their schools and hospitals, that a church can lawfully expel gay children from its schools for the simple fact of who they are. The false power of his lobby cows politicians when instead they should be brave.

Laws in this country carry any number of mutant clauses to respect the intolerance of churches. Slowly, the public view of this intolerance shifts. The worry for people such as Shelton is that the arrival of same-sex marriage might shift it more quickly. He has his finger in the dyke. In a last desperate gasp, he is arguing for the right to shout vilification through the hole.

Just colourful stuff

George Christensen has a problem with pamphlets. The last one to cause him trouble was a university magazine he happened to edit.

In it, he wrote a piece saying, among other things, "the truth is that women are bloody stupid". Another article complained that newer versions of the Bible were "removing accusations that the Jews killed Christ". Elsewhere was a joke about a gay man dying of AIDS.

This 1998 curio resurfaced during the 2010 election campaign. Christensen apologised, explaining that the bigotry was "in jest" and had only been brought to light by a Labor smear campaign.

Tony Abbott, who was then leader of the opposition, refused to rebuke Christensen. "There's colourful stuff from my uni days," was all he would say. "There's colourful stuff from Julia Gillard's uni days."

The problem for both men is they never outgrew the pettiness of those university days. They never outgrew the small-minded obsessions, the viciousness, the ill-informed hate.

Both Abbott and Christensen signed a petition this week to suspend funding for a program addressing the bullying of children on the basis of their sexuality. Abbott had no concerns about the program when he was leading the government that funded it. The program was raised in the party room, concerns were dismissed, and it went no further.

And that is the point. This mean little campaign is only in the most basic sense about ill-placed morality. What it is really about is splitting the party Malcolm Turnbull now leads. Uncertain children – bullied for their sexuality, more likely than others to attempt suicide, to be harassed or intimidated – are nothing more than collateral damage.

An independent review was conducted into the Safe Schools program. Unsurprisingly, it found little wrong with the initiative. The teaching of tolerance is difficult to argue against.

But the argument continues. The backbench petition is only part of that. Christensen used parliamentary privilege this week to suggest the program was written by a "paedophilia advocate". It was not. Earlier, he had said the materials mimicked the grooming technique of paedophiles.

This is a base slur, born of the oldest bigotries. It is about conflating homosexuality with paedophilia. It is disgusting in every way. Christensen should feel the shame of his idiocy. The words, if he had any decency, would sour in his mouth.

Instead, queer children have listened this week as their happiness and identity became the plaything of hateful politicians. They have heard as Christensen mocked their "gender confusion". They heard as he told anyone born with same-sex attraction that they should live a life without intimacy, a life in denial of who they are. "Someone makes the choice that they're going to have homosexual sex, that's up to them ... If you've chosen it or if you're born with it, the act is the act."

It does not take much to imagine what the cruelty of this debate might do to a child, but it does take empathy. Clearly, these men have none.

The right wing of the Coalition has been aided in this campaign by *The Australian* and fringe groups such as the Australian Christian Lobby. For them, it is about politics. For any decent person, it is about the vulnerable and marginalised. Any decent person would see how sick it is to play this group of children for advantage. But Christensen doesn't. Abbott doesn't. For them, no dignity is worth more than their own. It's still just a game. It's still just colourful stuff.

Culture bores

It is a curious thing when a tabloid newspaper chooses to put on its front page events of more than 200 years ago. It suggests a quixotic interpretation of the word "news".

Yet there on the front page of *The Daily Telegraph* this week was the news that Captain James Cook did not in fact "discover" Australia. This ran as an exclusive, under the headline "Whitewash".

In the interest of keeping readers up to date, the piece was accompanied by Nathaniel Dance-Holland's portrait of the explorer, painted some time in the mid-1770s.

"Students at a leading NSW university are being told to refer to Australia as having been 'invaded' instead of settled in a highly controversial rewriting of official Australian history," the story began. "They are also told it is offensive to suggest James Cook 'discovered' Australia and inappropriate to say the indigenous people have lived here for 40,000 years."

The only academic *The Daily Telegraph* could find for comment was Keith Windschuttle, best known for his denial of the Stolen Generations. "Under international law, Australia has always been regarded as a settled country according to the leading judgments in international law, both here and around the world," he said. "Until the law changes, there is no sound basis on which to say invaded. That is wrong."

The Institute of Public Affairs was also on hand to criticise the materials, saying they interfered with "the free flow of ideas".

It was later reported that the Queensland University of Technology used the same materials. The truth is, many universities do.

Asked about the material, Queensland premier Annastacia Palaszczuk said: "For many years Australian schools and Australian institutions have not told the truth about the way in which Australia was settled. A lot of Indigenous people lost their lives, there were massacres and the truth always must be told."

The Daily Telegraph reported her statement under the headline "Qld premier backs white invasion history".

The guidelines that so incensed *The Daily Telegraph* were in fact prepared in 1996. It does not take much work to find this out. It is written on them.

This material is not controversial. It is fact. It engages with the terms on which white people arrived in Australia. It engages with the fact that white settlement involved the dispossession of a people, sometimes by force, always by coercive policy.

But the issue here is larger. The issue is that instead of dealing with the modern reality of Indigenous Australia, we are dealing with outdated culture war. Instead of dealing with gaps in education and health and life expectancy, we are squabbling over language used in universities. Children in remote communities are committing suicide, and one of the country's largest newspapers is mocking the use of the term "Indigenous Australians" in preference to "Aborigines".

This is about distraction. It is about avoiding truth so as not to face up to it. It is about pretending White Australia's relationship with Indigenous people was settled in 1788 and that somehow the problems of Indigenous Australia are not Australia's problems. It is about pretending that these problems are not current, are not something faced every day.

It's much easier to jeer at the academe than to address chronic disadvantage. It is also an extraordinary waste of time. The awful reality, as reported on the front page of today's paper, is that it can also be an extraordinary waste of young life.

Please hold the line

The letter came from Michael Digges, the business manager at the Catholic Archdiocese of Sydney. He is a cheerful looking man in heavy spectacles and clashing patterns, the kind of person who keeps pens in his top pocket and appears innocuous, who doesn't know what to do with his face in photographs.

"You may be aware that the Catholic Archdiocese of Sydney is a significant user of goods and services from many corporations, both local and international," the letter began.

And later: "Undoubtedly, many of the Catholic population of Sydney would be your employees, customers, partners and suppliers. It is therefore with grave concern that I write to you about the Marriage Equality for Australians campaign."

The letter was sent to organisations that undersigned a newspaper advertisement supporting marriage equality, which ran in May and June last year.

The subtext was scarcely subtext at all: continue to publicly support marriage equality and the Catholic Church will boycott your services. Digges' jarring patterns were more a curdled logic.

After the letter was sent, the then chair of Telstra, Catherine Livingstone, was reportedly summoned to the offices of the Catholic Archbishop of Sydney, Anthony Fisher. Telstra holds multimillion-dollar contracts in Catholic schools. An insider told The Australian the company "did not want to risk its commercial relationship with the church".

At the meeting with Fisher, Telstra agreed to quietly back away from the campaign for marriage equality. This week, the company said it had "no further plans to be active in the debate".

The church has an ancient view of its primacy. It has an ancient view of marriage, too: described in Digges' letter as being "as it is now and has been over the millennia".

But it is out of step with society. Often, it is out of step with its own congregation. Many would be appalled to know that the church used its businesses – businesses built on tax exemptions – to secretly force companies into abandoning social causes.

A church that acts this way is a church of power rather than religion. It is the work not of a faith but a pressure group. It is a church poisoned by a high-handed executive, a church aware of its dwindling relevance, working in the shadows to maintain its import.

Telstra was wrong to step back from its support for marriage equality. It has stepped back from decency. The other businesses that signed up to the Australian Marriage Equality campaign last year would do well to step forward now and make their support vocal. They will be in agreement with the majority of Australians and with history.

And that is what is truly appalling. The church's view is a minority position. It has become the fringe on this issue. But the church's spectral power – in business, in politics – trades on a fear that continually overestimates its position.

In Digges' letter he characterises support for marriage equality as part of a "cashed-up, activist-driven media campaign". But it is nowhere near as cashed up as the medieval campaign run by the church; certainly, it is nowhere near as activist.

The next census will place "no religion" as the first option in its question about belief. Business and politics would be wise to do the same.

Show this mob doubt

It is a tradition in newspapers to editorialise on election day in favour of a political party. It is a quaint relic of media power, a belief that readers might be told how to vote, that they might be waiting for the grandiose pronouncement of a dozen unsigned column inches before exercising their suffrage.

In 2013, for instance, *The Sydney Morning Herald* endorsed Tony Abbott's opposition. The editorial reads now as a lesson in high farce. "Australia is crying out for a stable government that can be trusted to deliver what it promises," it began. "The *Herald* believes only the Coalition can achieve that within the limited mandate Tony Abbott will carry into office should he prevail on Saturday." The piece concluded: "The Coalition under Tony Abbott deserves the opportunity to return trust to politics."

In 2007 *The Australian* backed Kevin Rudd against John Howard. Again, the paper endorsed the very qualities their candidate lacked most: "we believe he has the administrative experience to manage constructive change". *The Daily Telegraph* thought so, too, and wrote: "This is an unusual editorial in that it praises the leadership and legacy of our current prime minister – and calls for him to be thrown out of office ... Kevin Rudd has shown discipline. He has campaigned with enthusiasm, ideas and energy. We believe that Kevin Rudd is the right man for these times."

After an eight-week campaign, *The Saturday Paper* makes no endorsement of either major party candidate. This is not because such an endorsement would be anachronistic or self-important, although it would be that too. It is because nowhere in this campaign has the vision of either party shown itself to be sufficiently brave or large or consistent as to warrant commendation.

Speaking at the National Press Club on Thursday, Malcolm Turnbull crystallised some of this malaise. He identified in Australians a desire for common purpose.

"I believe they want our parliament to offload the ideology, to end the juvenile theatrics and gotcha moments, to drop the personality politics," he said. "They want our focus to be on issues that matter to them – and an end to division for division's sake. Australians are entitled to expect that of their parliament ... My strong sense is that what Australians are looking for most from this election is a step up in political culture – strong, decisive, resolute leadership, yet with a focus on what unites rather than divides."

As ever, Turnbull is wonderful at articulating problems and apparently uninterested in solving them. He describes a parallel politics in which neither he nor Bill Shorten appear present. He was right in every half-sentence, which is why this campaign has been so wrong.

Labor's sensible reforms on negative gearing where cynically dismantled by the Coalition before they had even been properly described, as the Liberal Party's minor alterations to Medicare were by Labor. In the last weeks of the campaign a phoney war has been fought over costings and boats and a privatisation agenda that does not exist.

Much could have been explained to the voting public in eight weeks, but little was. Both major parties are to blame for this. The campaign was a conspiracy of distraction.

In not endorsing a candidate, however, *The Saturday Paper* does not say today's vote is unimportant. Australia faces significant challenges – economic, environmental and demographic – and badly needs for a government that can ably navigate these challenges.

Such a government was not apparent on the campaign trail. It can only be hoped it will be found in the parliament.

The Nauru files

The most damning part, the most appalling, were the six words Immigration Minister Peter Dutton spoke in his first interview following the leak of thousands of documents recording allegations of abuse on Nauru. The words were free of emotion and everything that is wrong with this situation. "Most of that's," Dutton said, "been reported before."

This is the reality in Australia. Abuse does not trouble ministers. It does not worry voters. We know about it. The political calculus says we do not care.

A child is beaten by a guard, their throat held, their face smashed against the ground, a chair thrown at them, and we do not care.

A parent made desperate by mistreatment plans to carry their children beneath the waves, to die with their family, and we do not care.

A girl under 10, a victim of sexual abuse, undresses and encourages a group of adults to violate her, and we do not care.

Prime Minister Malcolm Turnbull says these people, people we sent to Nauru and for whose indefinite detention we are paying, are the responsibility of the Nauru government. He ignores the calls for a royal commission. He leaves it to a failed state, a state that expelled its judiciary and its coroner, to investigate the lives we ruin there.

Scott Morrison, who was immigration minister when much of this abuse was reported, simply says: "It's important to stress that incident reports of themselves aren't a reporting of fact; they are reporting that an allegation has been made of a particular action."

The Nauru files, reported by *The Guardian*, are a logbook of desperation. Each word is another obscenity scratched into the history of this country's refugee policy. Everywhere but here, these reports draw condemnation.

The UNHCR called for the immediate removal of asylum seekers from Nauru. It saw these reports as "a progressive deterioration of the situation of refugees and asylum seekers".

The Australian Medical Association called for the establishment of an independent investigative body, removed from government, to inquire into the situation.

The senior director for research at Amnesty International, Anna Neistat, said: "The Australian government has engaged in one of the most successful mass cover-ups I've witnessed in my career of documenting human rights violations. They've repeatedly said this kind of abuse has not been going on. They've been lying."

The government knows about this abuse but it does not care. The public knows, too. Dutton is correct when he says much of this has already been reported. He is wrong when he mistakes this for an excuse. If anything, it makes it worse.

Some suffering is ignored because it is difficult. Society turns away from Indigenous disadvantage because the issue is complex and the solutions unclear. The treatment of refugees is not like that. The solution is simple: bring these people to Australia.

Yet for decades Australia has been told not to care for these people. It has been told they are terrorists, queue jumpers, bludgers who will take your jobs. Politicians have won elections demonising them. The public has decided not to care. People die in these camps, victims of our callousness.

One day, a prime minister will apologise to the people we hurt in offshore detention. One day we will say sorry to the boys and girls whose childhoods we stole, to the parents we drove mad, to the young men and women who tried to kill themselves to halt the unending cruelty of their lives.

We will say sorry for the things we knew. We will say sorry and hope that we never again treat people the way we treated refugees. We will talk in hushed voices about the shame of the politics under which we currently live. Ministers like Dutton and Morrison will be named for their barbarism.

One day we will say sorry and face up to the racist indifference with which we police our borders. Hopefully that day is not so far away.

Behind high walls

There is no sign to mark the turnoff to Cleveland Youth Detention Centre in Townsville. The road that snakes in front of it is only guttered on one side. The bitumen breaks away to the left, into the dry earth of a vacant block. This is a forgotten place.

Inside, behind high wire fences, is another sorry chapter in our treatment of young prisoners.

A boy sits at a table, refusing to shower. He is neither abusive nor intimidating. A staff member radios for back-up. Fourteen people respond. Five guards force the boy to the ground, cuff his hands and ankles. One guard uses a Hoffman rescue knife to cut his clothes from his body. The tool is designed to cut down people after they have hanged themselves.

The boy is left for an hour, naked and shackled. Five days earlier, he had attempted suicide. The on-call manager erroneously describes him as "extremely aggressive".

In the past year, children here have attempted suicide 31 times. The reports describe "ligatures around their necks".

Elsewhere in the centre, eight Indigenous children are held in isolation for 10 days. For the first 48 hours, they are not allowed to leave their cells. For the remaining eight days, they are locked up and alone for stretches of 22 hours.

At the prison's swimming pool, private guards arrive with an unmuzzled dog on a long leash. As a girl tries to get out of the pool, the guard lets out the leash. The dog runs forward, barking, pulled up onto its hind legs. Apparently these private guards do not have authority to touch the children.

In searches, it is alleged, guards force children to undergo a program of "squatting and lifting" banned in adult prisons. Young girls are told to lift their breasts for inspection; young boys to hold up their genitals as they squat down and are checked.

Another prisoner is mocked for his skin, a child humiliated by adult guards. "They used to call me 'black dog', 'caged monkey', 'abo'. All sorts of filthy names. 'Motherfucker.' It used to hurt me."

He says he was beaten until it hurt to stand. He says a guard spat in his food, then called through on an intercom to taunt him with this fact.

There is closed-circuit television footage of some of this abuse. The Queensland Youth Detention Inspectorate has inquired into other parts.

A recommendation was made to review the treatment of the boy cuffed and stripped naked by guards. The centre responded that it did not have the staff to carry out the investigation.

The government knows about this mistreatment. These accounts are drawn from reports sitting on its desks. They are only public because they have been released under freedom of information laws.

There is a crisis in youth detention in this country, a crisis of numbers and of conditions. A generation of prisoners – too many of them, and too many of them First Australians – are being brutalised by a system in a state of deep dysfunction.

Cleveland Youth Detention Centre is not a rogue institution, just as Don Dale in the Northern Territory is not unique in its cruelty. Both facilities reflect the realities of youth incarceration.

The difference is that Australia has now seen over their high walls. We have been confronted by a punitive system apparently built to protect us. It is a reminder of how cynically narrow the royal commission announced last month really was.

No doubt there are fiendish problems among the young people who find themselves imprisoned. But those problems are made only worse by a system that tortures children, that punishes instead of rehabilitates. We have to ask, is it worth it?

Hanson cad

It is ironic that Pauline Hanson began her second maiden speech with the word "welcome" – except that irony requires a wit beyond her possession.

Hanson is this country's jittering id. Her speech to the senate on Wednesday pulsed with a sickly paranoia, a world view contorted by victimhood.

"If we do not make changes now, there will be no hope in the future," Hanson warned. "Have no doubt that we will be living under sharia law and treated as second-class citizens with second-class rights if we keep heading down the path with the attitude, 'She'll be right, mate.'"

Hanson's cry is for a ban on Muslim immigration, a ban on headscarves, a ban on Halal certification, a ban on the construction of mosques and Muslim schools, and the unspecified surveillance of those that already exist "until the present crisis is over".

In Hanson's Australia, migrants are taking the dole or are offered government jobs ahead of others. They are responsible for hospital waiting queues, for the crowding of schools, for house prices, for road traffic, for lack of water.

Welfare, in Hanson's mind, is exploited by Muslim men with multiple wives having more and more children to increase their benefit payments. "How many have ever held a job? Why would anyone want to work when welfare is so very lucrative?"

For Hanson, there are no qualifiers. Islam is evil. It is a colonising ideology bent on remaking our culture. Its women are oppressed. Its men are violent. "How many lives will be lost or destroyed," she asked, "trying to determine who is good and who is bad?"

In the 20 years and four days since her first maiden speech – a time separated by multiple failed election bids and prison – Hanson has only become more inflammatory and more bigoted. Her speech was 30 minutes of unsourced anxiety.

It was full of specious declarations, variations on the claim that "globalisation, economic rationalism, free trade and ethnic diversity has seen our country's decline". It was a screed against "the mantras of diversity or tolerance".

Hanson's speech was not a tissue of lies so much as a phonebook. But the great lie, the one that gave dignity to her other lies, was the lie of secularism. "The separation of church and state has become an essential component of our way of life," she said, "and anything that threatens that separation threatens our freedom."

This is a worthy principle, but it is not one Hanson defends.

Nowhere does she mention the illegal payments made by the Abbott government to the school chaplaincy program. Nowhere does she mention the influence of church groups on issues such as same-sex marriage or euthanasia, issues in which the clouding of church and state produces policy at odds with the will of the public.

Hanson pretends the cloak of secularism to cover her real bigotry, to generalise a target that is deeply specific. "Islam does not believe in democracy, freedom of speech, freedom of the press, or freedom of assembly," she says without evidence. "It does not separate religion and politics. It is partly a religion, but it is much more than that. It has a political agenda that goes far outside the realm of religion."

There is an argument that says Hanson's views should be left unreported. This view correctly argues that her first maiden speech changed Australia, that it permitted and emboldened an expedient racism. But it incorrectly argues that Hanson's views are only amplified by interrogation.

Hanson is wrong. In being wrong, she harms an entire community. She demonises women in headscarves, mothers in prayer rooms, young men in mosques. But the only way to counter her wrong is to reject it, to examine it, to explain to her and to those who follow her the error of their prejudice. Silence will not answer Hanson. And she must be answered. It is in the darkness of silence that her paranoia grows.

In the next six years – a period about which she gloats in her speech – Hanson will be a conductor for all manner of division and intolerance. It is too easy to leave these intolerances unexamined because of their self-evident incorrectness, to allow Hanson to make unchecked claims because their entire basis is so unserious. Yet each small thing Hanson says should be checked and corrected. Her rejection by this country should be one of mounting counterpoint. It should start with the malformed conspiracy theories and half-truths from which Wednesday's fanciful speech was cobbled. Surely, in 20 years, this country has matured to a point where it owes itself that.

Eject Dutton

There was grim calculation to Peter Dutton's statement. He had sought a brief for his bigotry and had one prepared. "The advice I have," he told the parliament, "is that out of the last 33 people who have been charged with terrorist-related offences in this country, 22 of those people are from second- and third-generation Lebanese Muslim background."

The comment followed his earlier criticism of Malcolm Fraser's immigration policy – the repudiation of the humanity of, perhaps, his party's last decent leader. "The reality," he said, "is Malcolm Fraser did make mistakes in bringing some people in the 1970s and we're seeing that today."

The undertow to this was payback for Fraser's criticism of the Liberal Party over its treatment of refugees, culminating in his resignation from the party prior to his death last year. The Coalition will forever feel betrayed by a man who held to his values as his party drifted away from them.

Dutton calls this an "honest discussion". He says, "I have been factual in what I said and I want to make sure that we have the best possible country."

Turnbull refused to confront his immigration minister. Not content with lying once, he lied three times. He called Dutton a "thoughtful, committed and compassionate immigration minister".

Andrew Laming said Dutton was speaking only the "prima facie truth" of immigration. This is a nonsense. Dutton was using the conduct of 22 people in an attempt to demonise an entire people. He was doing so cynically and with the sharpest cruelty.

Dutton is desperate for this to become a culture war. He hopes that his racism will wedge Labor. "Bill Shorten can carry on being part of the tricky elite in this country," he said. "He can talk double-code to people, he can be tricky in his language. I'm not going to be intimidated by it."

For Dutton, this is a game. Yet the impact of this rhetoric is real. Following his comments, Anne Aly, the first Muslim woman elected to the parliament, began receiving racist emails.

"Peter Dutton was right," read one, with the subject line "Leb thugs". "Pack your bags and piss off back to where you came from and take all of your terrorist faith with you."

On Aly's Facebook page, another threat: "I would love to kill you and poison your family."

And another: "Your a worthless cancer on this country you and your Koran can fuck off the sooner your dead the better this place will be. ALL MUSLIMS WILL DIE."

This is Dutton's Australia. It is an Australia where his influence depends on disharmony, where his cling to power requires the punishment of an innocent people.

Dutton should have been sacked long ago. He should have been sacked for incompetence, for his inability to resolve the crisis on Manus and Nauru. He should have been sacked for lying about the intentions of a woman who was raped on Nauru, who was spirited from a hospital bed as she waited for an abortion required by that rape.

He should have been sacked for his fallacious claim that refugee advocates are responsible for the self-harm to which indefinite detention drives asylum seekers, or for his misleading commentary regarding spying on a Greens senator. He should have been sacked 1600 times over, once for each of the people doomed in offshore detention. But he was not.

Dutton is Turnbull's disgrace. Each outrage is a test of the prime minister's gormlessness. With each refusal to act decently, with each refusal to quiet Dutton's obscenities, he shows more and more his inability to lead.

Dutton should be sacked. If Turnbull cannot do this, he should reflect on what his own lust for power is doing to the country he once dreamt of leading.

Milo and POTUS

It was always a question of when. That is the way with a poseur: the act can never be sustained, not forever.

The inevitable collapse of Milo Yiannopoulos's career is the beginning, it can be hoped, of a larger collapse in the ill-formed movement of which he was a figurehead. His public disintegration stems from the truth that binds him to the alt-right: that he is fundamentally unserious, and so are they.

Yiannopoulos lost a $250,000 book contract and his job as an editor at the extremist website *Breitbart* after a live-streamed conversation from last year surfaced this week, showing him condoning paedophilia. He described sex with minors as "coming-of-age relationship ... in which those older men help those younger boys discover who they are".

He later apologised in a self-aggrandising press conference. "I've never apologised for anything else before," he said. "I don't anticipate doing it again."

Yiannopoulos is the crossover star from the internet's ugly fringe. The Southern Poverty Law Centre called him "the person who propelled the alt-right movement into the mainstream".

Yiannopoulos came to prominence in an internet movement that targeted and harassed women involved in online gaming. His are the politics of opportunism. He took the lessons of "gamergate" and teased them into a persona of vicious cunning.

Yet there was never any real substance to him. Like the alt-right he represented, there was no next: there was only the desire to destroy the now. He could recant his views because they had no depth, no underpinning. The same is true of Donald Trump.

The British writer Laurie Penny offered this description, after attending a party with Yiannopoulos at the Republican convention: "It's the game of turning raw rage into political currency, the unscrupulous whorebaggery of the troll gone pro. These are people who cashed in their limited principles to cheat at poker. Milo is the best player here."

Political movements require philosophies. Their leaders earn that distinction by the thinking they have done. The alt-right has no such leaders. Instead, they had Yiannopoulos – a message board charlatan, bleached the colour of Instagram and dressed in his Aunt Pam's pearls.

Yiannopoulos is a bigot, a hateful clown. His one skill is publicity, which his supporters mistake for insight. Even as he attempted contrition this week, he could not help but mention "the level of interest, the sheer number of people who love me".

Vanity is a marker of the figures who have bubbled to the surface of the alt-right. Their interest is themselves, not the people they purport to represent. Trump is Yiannopoulos with a different number hair dye.

The alt-right is not a political movement in any conventional sense. It is an expression of confused anger, a cry that now heard will fade.

That anger will have to be addressed. Politics has before it an enormous task. Yet it will not be addressed by the hucksters and spivs who in the meantime seek to profit from its anguish.

This is not the end of Yiannopoulos, just as Trump will not end with his presidency. But it is the breaking apart of an inchoate expediency that plays with the world like a children's toy.

Inhuman services

A month ago next week, *The Saturday Paper* reported on the death of Rhys Cauzzo. The florist and musician was being pursued by Centrelink over historic payments. He was menaced by debt collectors. On January 26, he committed suicide. His mother and girlfriend say Centrelink's treatment of him tipped him over the edge.

This week the secretary of the Department of Human Services, Kathryn Campbell, was asked by a senate committee about Cauzzo's death. Her response was so specious, so tellingly disconnected, that it is worth reproducing at some length. To paraphrase would be to inject feeling.

"This is a very sad event, and we don't want to make it harder for families," she said. "This was a former recipient. It wasn't a current recipient. So that's why the debt collectors had been used on that occasion. There are always different dimensions to stories that appear in the media, as I'm sure you're aware. We have a different take on what was reported.

"We provided the initiating letter. And the initiating letter asked people to clarify. There was a 1800 number that people were able to access, and deal with and work through those issues. We often find that people are distressed when dealing with the social welfare system. I mean, every morning I have a look at my email and there are a number of emails about people who are distressed in different circumstances – it may be their personal circumstances, it may be the interaction of our system with other systems, it may sometimes be a misunderstanding of eligibility under the criteria. And we work with those individuals to try and resolve those issues ... But this is a complex payment system. And often people don't understand the obligations that go with the payments, that they are required to update various pieces of information. And we do our very best to make it as streamlined and user-friendly as possible. But I do acknowledge that there will be people distressed.

"I think in the lead-up to Christmas and into January people became even more distressed because of the significant media attention around these issues. I think half of the stories that appeared in the media were not part of this system – they were general debt matters. And because of some of the stories in the media, there was a belief that all debts were wrong. And therefore people started to get saying, 'I want this debt waived. I don't think I should have to pay this back.'"

None of what Campbell said changed the facts of Cauzzo's death – it simply avoided them. This is not about the media. It is not about whether a debt was raised manually or by a grossly flawed algorithm. It is about a department completely unwilling to engage with the brutality of its procedures.

Recently, private information about welfare recipients has been leaked to the media in the hope of discrediting critics. After *The Saturday Paper* published Rhys Cauzzo's story, the department shared his personal data with our reporter in the hope of changing the piece. This week, Barnaby Joyce said: "If you want to keep your information absolutely private, don't go and get the dole whilst you've also got a job."

The contempt in which people who receive welfare are held is the contempt of a government out of touch with its responsibilities. It is this contempt that designs a system such as the one that drove Rhys Cauzzo to suicide.

Welfare does not exist to punish people; it exists to help them. In receiving the support of the state, a person does not forfeit their ordinary rights. Nor should they.

These simple principles seem beyond this government and beyond the department that serves it. In their place is a deadly barbarism, a breakdown of the social compact under which this country once operated. Our system of social security was once the envy of the world. Under this government, it has become a monster.

On Bill Leak

Bill Leak was a racist. To pretend otherwise is a nonsense. His death doesn't change that. The culture warring obituaries don't change that. The misguided plea of a former prime minister still squaring up against the national broadcaster doesn't change that.

It was racism that drew a cartoon of two Aboriginal men drinking as they read about John Howard's Northern Territory intervention. "Rape's out, bashing's out," the speech bubble read. "This could set our culture back by 2000 years!.."

It was racism that drew a cartoon of two Aboriginal men drinking as a woman slumped battered behind them. Blood ran from her head and nose. A comedy of stars circled above her. The speech bubble: "Sheilas! You give 'em an enriching cultural experience and what thanks do you get??!!.."

They were the same men in both cartoons. For Leak, they were always the same men – grotesqueries of a culture his pictures deemed subhuman.

Bill Leak was not brave. There is nothing brave about the persecution of minorities. There is nothing brave about tracing clichés. Leak became a martyr for free speech but in reality he was a martyr for the right to be wrong.

Leak's late-career targets were rarely the powerful. At some point he gave up on genuine insight. About the same time, he gave up on being funny.

There is history to these cartoons. It is the history of a kind of racism that would not be published in another developed democracy anywhere in the world. Leak's late cartoons drew on the tropes of colonial propaganda to demean and dehumanise an entire race of people. That was before you got to the homophobia or the Islamophobia or any of the paranoias that drove his pen.

Bill Leak drew for a country that no longer exists. The majority of the words written since his death have been a kind of specious voodoo – a hope that Leak's Australia could somehow be reanimated, that racist intimidation would once again dominate, that freedom of speech may be co-opted as a tool to keep down the future and the diversity of people who will make it.

The Australian's editor-at-large, Paul Kelly, wrote this week that Leak represented "a nation at war over its core values". He called him "an iconic figure in this struggle … the most important local symbol in the cultural disruption afflicting Western societies." Leak's bigotry, in Kelly's mind, was a corrective to the progressives "dismantling the cultural norms and traditions that have made Western societies such as Australia so successful".

These are bizarre assertions. They depend on the repression of minorities to maintain an ailing status quo. That is what Leak spent his time doing.

There is nothing to celebrate in Bill Leak's death. There was little to celebrate in the last years of his cartoons, either.

A day in court

This is not a piece about guilt. A court will decide that. This is a piece about a church that is finally being forced to address accusations of child abuse where they should always have been addressed: under the law.

The details of the charges laid against George Pell are not yet known. Victoria Police's deputy commissioner, Shane Patton, confirmed they were multiple and that they related to historical sexual abuse allegations. "There are," he said, "multiple complainants relating to those charges."

We know about some of the accusations that have been made against Pell in the past. The church investigated them. Its reports cleared the cardinal. He maintained his innocence.

After he was charged by police on Thursday, Pell made a statement that he intended to return to Australia. He was consulting a doctor, having earlier insisted he was too sick to travel.

"There has been relentless character assassination for months … I am looking forward finally to having my day in court. I am innocent of these charges. They are false," he said.

"I've kept Pope Francis, the Holy Father, regularly informed during these long months and have spoken to him on a number of occasions in the last week, most recently a day or so ago … All along I have been completely consistent and clear in my total rejection of these allegations. News of these charges strengthens my resolve and court proceedings now offer an opportunity to clear my name and return back to work."

Pell is the third-highest-ranking Catholic in the Vatican. He is the most senior Vatican official to have been charged with child sexual offences. The events of this week will deeply unsettle the church.

Child abuse has remade the church in a way once unimaginable. It has taken the moral authority of its hierarchy, laid bare its hypocrisies. It has emptied pews and bankrupted parishes.

The church has presided over this collapse for one reason above all others: it has sought to put itself outside the law. In civil matters, it has organised ludicrous corporate structures to protect itself from litigation. It has built parallel processes to keep itself from accountability. Where it has used the law, it has used it to harass victims, even after determining the veracity of their abuse.

It is in this context that George Pell has been charged. He has become and is likely to remain a symbol of the church's relationship with the law.

In announcing the charges, Patton said: "The process and procedures that are being followed in the charging of Cardinal Pell have been the same that have been applied in a whole range of historical sex offences, whenever we investigate them ... Cardinal Pell has been treated the same as anyone else in this investigation."

This last point is an important one. It is not just about Pell; it is about all priests. It could have saved the church its collapse.

Justice for Elijah

There is red ochre spread on the windows of the Supreme Court. There are protests in Melbourne and Sydney and Canberra and Kalgoorlie and Adelaide and Brisbane.

The signs read "Justice for Elijah" and "Black lives matter" and "Sorry means you don't do it again". A woman says: "This is blood on the Commonwealth."

Meyne Wyatt, a relative of Elijah Doughty, says: "You're treating us like we're animals. We're not animals. We're people. You're killing us."

Elijah Doughty was 14. The man who killed him was white. A white jury found that his death was not manslaughter. It was a lesser charge: dangerous driving causing death. The man who killed him was sentenced to three years' jail. He will likely be released early, perhaps next year.

The judge described the need for "a penalty which properly reflects the value which our community places upon the sanctity of human life". He said the man's "unblemished record is clearly a mitigating factor which I do take into account and to which I give full weight".

The man who killed Elijah Doughty drove to a reserve looking for him. When he died, Doughty was riding a motorcycle stolen from the man's property. The man had chased him in a car. In the pursuit down a dirt track, he ran over the boy and killed him.

The man attempted to resuscitate Elijah, but he was already dead. Later, he told police: "I just wanted my kids' motorbike. It was in a locked container in our yard with two dogs with it … We came here for a good future. We didn't come here for this. We didn't come here to have motorbikes stolen, padlocks broken."

In the months before Elijah's death, vigilantes in Kalgoorlie-Boulder were calling for violent retribution against Indigenous people suspected of stealing. It is not clear if the man who killed Elijah knew of this.

One post, a day after Elijah's death, read: "I'm sorry, but fuck that Elijah kid. He had a criminal history, should have been in juvenile correction but because of his skin tone and family background he wasn't. He chose to steal the bike. He chose the repercussions. The guy charged with manslaughter had no intention of killing the stupid cunt but it fucking happened."

The death of Elijah Doughty is a signal moment. In pondering the value of a human life, the judge asked the community to do the same. He asked unintentional questions, too: Is a black life worth less than a white one? Does this country grieve the same now as if a white boy were run down on a city street?

The answers to these questions are grim. They involve a national culpability. This moment is the moment that we ask the truest nature of the relationship between white and black Australia. There is a test here for this country: Are we better than our history?

"It's white people killing us," the playwright Nakkiah Lui wrote this week. "Only white people can stop it. Aboriginal people don't have an 'issue' with white people. We aren't killing you. White people have an issue with us. White people have an issue with perpetrating homicide. White people have a problem with their culture being built and sustained on structural murder ... Your culture is murdering. Your culture is killing. It's not in the past, because it's still happening, and as long as it continues to happen, you are all responsible for it. How about you all start taking responsibility for your white violence because you all benefit from it. Every single one of you."

One man was on trial for the death of Elijah Doughty, but it is the whole country that is now in the dock. The charge sheet is long and unhappy and if we are to heal as a nation it must be reckoned with.

A life given to failure

The important thing to remember about Tony Abbott is that nobody wanted him. Whenever he intervenes in public debate, this fact should overwhelm all others.

It was by accident that he was ever leader: a single vote, determined after Joe Hockey's clod-handed intervention in the ballot. When Abbott won the 2013 election, he did so in spite of himself. The Coalition triumphed over his deep and sustained unpopularity.

Tony Abbott is a champion of lost causes, none more so than himself. When he joined the National Civic Council at university, the Democratic Labor Party was already a spent force. His first great political mentor, B.A. Santamaria, was preaching the end of days without realising that only his were over. Ever since, Abbott has given his life to failed institutions.

In Tony Abbott's mind, he is the vanquished leader of a silent majority. In reality, he is a fringe figure who has spent his life clinging to the leftovers of debates other people have won.

There is a simple reason for his unpopularity: very few people want what he wants. The Australia of his imagination is largely uninhabitable. It is a place of exclusion and nihilistic priorities. This is quite deliberate. Power for people such as Abbott is about disenfranchising anyone who is not like them. Theirs is a fantasy of simple values and white convention. The great struggle of Abbott's life is that it is happening in the present.

When he says he will cross the floor on energy policy, it is not because the Liberal Party has betrayed itself. It is because he never belonged in it. There is no real place for a person such as Abbott in contemporary society, which is why he is still in the parliament. Business would not have him and nor would the community sector. The church in which he first discovered his failings could not find room for him among its charities.

Abbott is a man contemptuous of the planet on which he lives. He is fearful of equality and totally unfeeling in his rejection of it.

The tragedy of this is that Abbott will forever have the imprimatur of the office he improbably held. His lies are held as truths because people in his position are not supposed to lie.

He says: "There is a big agenda here for many of the people behind same-sex marriage. This is the thin end of the wedge, that's why we should think long and hard before we vote and I certainly think the only safe course is to vote 'No'."

He says: "If things are as bad as this before same-sex marriage has happened, just think how much worse it could be in this brave new world the politically correct left would force on us."

Tony Abbott is smart enough to know that this is nonsense. He doesn't care. The problem for a man so used to being on the losing side is that he will do anything to win. He cares for nothing but himself.

Talk of shame

Peter Dutton says there are a lot of people who "have made a lot of mischief over a long period of time". It's true, but not in the way Dutton means it.

He does not argue when Ray Hadley says the first refugees to leave Manus for resettlement in the United States, "looked like a fashion show on a catwalk somewhere in Paris or New York".

Instead, he lies. He begins an argument about these refugees being economic migrants, despite two separate processes now assessing them to be refugees. He puts at risk a fragile deal to make a cheap point about the legitimacy of people he knows to be legitimate.

"There are a lot of people that haven't come out of war-ravaged areas," he says. "They're economic refugees. They got on a boat, paid a people smuggler a lot of money. And, you know, somebody once said to me that the world's biggest collection of Armani jeans and handbags [was] up on Nauru waiting for, you know, waiting for people to collect it when they depart."

Dutton knows this is a lie, but it doesn't trouble him. Either he is so used to lying on this issue that it has become his default, or he sees the margin of grubby advantage in it and has no hesitation in exploiting that.

"The reality is that these people have, at the generosity of the Australian taxpayer, received an enormous amount of support for a long period of time," he says. "We didn't ask people to hop on the boats. And we're getting them out, including through this US deal. But we have been taken for a ride, I believe, by a lot of the advocates and people within Labor and the Greens who want you to believe that, you know, this is a terrible existence. These photos demonstrate otherwise. People have seen photos in recent weeks of, you know, those up on Manus out enjoying themselves outside of the centre, by the beach and all the rest of it. Quickly they take down the photos from their Facebook pages when they're discovered, but there is a very different scenario up on Nauru and Manus than people want you to believe."

It is difficult to know what Dutton means when he talks about "all the rest of it".

Perhaps he means the suicides or the child abuse. Perhaps he means the days without proper sanitation.

Perhaps it's the makeshift tents in which children have lost their childhoods. Perhaps it's the women denied abortions or the pregnancies produced by rapes.

Perhaps he means the self-immolation or the murder by paid guards. Perhaps he means the mental anguish, the loss of hope, the calculated destruction of a few thousand lives for the sake of political gain.

The pictures of refugees leaving Manus Island are pictures of resilience. They are pictures of men with nothing but the backpacks they wheel in front of them, men who have survived what will one day be regarded as the great disgrace of this country's past 50 years. To Hadley and Dutton, they do not look desperate enough.

There are other photographs, which Dutton doesn't mention. There is the picture of Hamed Shamshiripour, dead in a forest, his eyes blacked out, his body shown as if after a lynching. There is the picture of Reza Barati, the last one his parents will ever see. There is the picture of Omid Masoumali, alight, calling for the world to end this.

Dutton does not mention these pictures because he does not care. He has presided over torture, and he does not care. He celebrates an incomplete solution, and mocks the men involved, because he does not care. All the rest of it is the stuff he doesn't think about. All the rest of it is this nation's unending shame.

Against the poor

The government's response is that it doesn't care. It will not suspend its flawed system of debt collection. It defends its actions in inaccurately and inappropriately raising thousands of debts against Australians. It feels no contrition or need to apologise.

It has taken three months for the government to respond to the senate report into the robo-debt fiasco. In doing so, it has dismissed complaints made against the system as "third parties ... aimed solely at scoring political points".

This is the system that, by the government's own estimates, claimed incorrect debts against at least 20,000 people. It is the system that began pursuing debts even as they were contested, that sooled private debt collectors on thousands of people.

It is the system built on an algorithm the government knew was flawed, that was used as a means of vindictiveness against vulnerable people.

Before the inquiry, the government acted to suppress critics. It and the department leaked private information about detractors. So fearful were some welfare recipients of explaining their experience that evidence had to be given in camera.

This is a system that cannot be defended, but the government defends it.

"The government is committed to maintaining a strong social welfare safety net. This requires that there be integrity in the welfare system," its response said.

"Each person should receive exactly what they are entitled to, no more and no less. This principle has been in place under successive governments and has not changed."

The government doesn't care about the flaws in this system because the government doesn't care about the people it serves.

It does not trouble the government that this system is needlessly vindictive. It does not trouble the government that error is its most consistent marker.

The cruelty of it is part of the design. The system of recovery exists to reinforce the view that welfare recipients are predisposed to fraud.

A society that does not wish to support the needy makes crimes of their need. This system makes criminals out of those who owe nothing. It falsely accuses thousands and then asks them to prove their innocence.

In any other portfolio, a system so delinquent, so bent by inaccuracy, would be immediately discontinued. There would be no excuse to keep it running.

But the government keeps this running because it says one thing: the concerns of the poor will not bend the government's resolve.

It does not matter that the sums recovered are inconsequential in comparison with the hardship unfairly wrought. Those errors are necessary to prove the government right.

To reject the senate inquiry is to reject fact. It is in this state of vicious fantasy that the government now routinely operates.

One-eyed bandits

It is not right to say Crown operates without laws. It is truer to say that laws are made for Crown.

Under the terms of its licensing agreement in Victoria, the state will pay compensation to the casino should any measure to combat problem gambling affect profits. For the next 33 years, the state is liable for payments up to $200 million to Crown for losses related to lowered betting limits, precommitment technology, restricted access to cash machines, or any other recommended policy to treat the addiction of gambling.

Under the same deal, which locks in Crown's licence until 2050, the casino managed to reduce its tax obligations. It pays no "super tax" on international and interstate VIP gaming.

Crown also got an extra 128 poker machine licences, 40 more tables on the casino floor and 50 additional automated game terminals.

In a statement to the stock exchange when the deal was done in 2014, Crown Resorts chairman James Packer said it corrected "a major competitive disadvantage on the issue of taxation".

In Sydney, Packer's harbour casino defies planning laws. The state's "unsolicited bid" provisions allowed for it to be conceived without independent evaluation. Special legislation was still needed, and The Casino Control (Amendment) Bill was passed. In effect, as Anne Davies wrote in *The Saturday Paper*, "… James Packer was awarded a restricted gaming licence for a VIP casino on publicly owned land without tender".

This week, Andrew Wilkie tabled tapes in parliament alleging Crown had serially conspired to increase its profits from poker machines. Moreover, Wilkie alleged, the Victorian regulator knew of tampering but did not take action. It simply directed that rigged machines be repaired.

Whistleblowers working with Wilkie claimed they had been directed to reset machines so as to reduce returns to players, taking down the mandated proportion of winnings. They said buttons on machines had been disabled to force higher bets and that other machines had their buttons shaved down so gamblers could jam them and cause the machine to play continuously, again increasing Crown's takings.

The whistleblowers allege a conspiracy to avoid anti-fraud and money laundering regulations. They say the casino papered over domestic violence and allowed gamblers to play until they soiled themselves, offering new clothes so they could keep going.

For what it's worth, Crown denies these stories. It "rejects the allegations made today under parliamentary privilege ... concerning the improper manipulation of poker machines and other illegal or improper conduct at Crown Casino in Melbourne". It "calls on Mr Wilkie to immediately provide to the relevant authorities all information relating to the matters alleged".

An inquiry will now begin. On trial will be extraordinary corporate greed. Even without Wilkie's allegations, Crown is a business running in a kind of moral vacuum, supported by subservient governments.

In a just world, the inquiry would not be limited simply to machine tampering and rapacious conduct. It would extend to the special relationship between governments and casinos.

These relationships are not only personal – although there is that, too, with a payroll that has included Tony Abbott's chief of staff, Peta Credlin; Labor national secretary Karl Bitar; senator Mark Arbib; Howard government minister Helen Coonan.

It is not just money, either – although there are millions of dollars in state revenue and hundreds of thousands of dollars in political donations

The relationship is about a curious orthodoxy regarding casinos. Politics behaves as if it needs them. It has no appetite for regulation. It has refused decades of advocacy for reform.

That is why licences are given with extraordinary concessions, why planning laws are modified or public lands leased for dollar coins. It is why you can smoke in gaming rooms.

Casinos have always been there and always will be, this logic goes. They are a necessary evil.

Wilkie's revelations bring this odd relationship into focus. Irrespective of what is found regarding Crown, they should ask a fundamental question: Why do governments do so much for casinos, and get so little in return?

The man with no face

In the dream he has no face. He is sitting on a couch, leaning forward as if to adjust something on a coffee table. When he looks up, he is the dead man from the photograph. He is Hamed Shamshiripour.

He is wearing the same pink polo shirt, the same loose blue trousers. His arms are thin almost to wasting and his head is shaved bald. His empty eyes, from the last photograph ever taken of him, eclipse what would otherwise have been his features. Unmistakably, he is dead.

I have been having this dream since August, when Hamed killed himself. At the time, we chose not to publish this photograph. His family found it too distressing.

We wrote that it looked like the scene of a lynching, and that it was. We wrote that his shoulders hung as if responding to a question for which there was no answer. We wrote that the Australian government was responsible for his death.

Hamed killed himself after he had been assessed as a refugee. He killed himself after Border Force's chief medical officer had been made aware of his dire mental state. He killed himself after Australia had refused to honour his wishes to be returned to the country he was fleeing.

Hamed Shamshiripour killed himself because he could not escape the hell Australia had made for him. He killed himself because he was trapped in the evil of our politics and no one in power cared enough to know he was there.

There is no more "in spite of". There is no longer any way a humane person could vote for the Labor or Liberal parties without giving thought to their position on refugees. This policy is bipartisan. The torture that killed Hamed Shamshiripour is the work of successive governments, elected by voters able to overlook their cruelty.

The men on Manus Island have been abandoned. That did not start this month, when power and sanitation was cut at the detention centre where they have been marooned. It didn't start this week, when soldiers began pulling apart what is left of the structure.

It started in 1992, when the concept of mandatory detention criminalised the legal act of seeking asylum. It started in 2001, with the *Tampa* and children overboard, when John Howard decided elections could be won on a fear of "boat people". It started with Kim Beazley's cowardice and Kevin Rudd's ambition and Julia Gillard's fecklessness, with Tony Abbott's cruelty and Malcolm Turnbull's impotence. It started a hundred different times and has been played out over and over.

What is happening on Manus Island is the real cost of the cynicism of our politics. The lives of these men have been traded for votes. They represent the comfort of this country and its fear.

The abandonment of these men is transactional. Their torture no longer serves a purpose. Voters do not blame them for traffic congestion and hospital waiting queues, as they once did, and so the government has lost interest in them. They are being killed with indifference.

Politics in this country has created a moral vacuum. It is not until we start voting on the issue of refugees, instead of voting despite it, that this will change.

The government is unmoved by the crisis on Manus. It is unconcerned by deaths such as Hamed's, by the broken defiance of his final moments. It has already forgotten the men left behind.

When the country votes, it has to remember this. It has to wake up from the nightmare.

Church and fate

When the royal commission sat for the final time, the church was not there. Senior figures were not present. It fell to a layperson to attend, to Francis Sullivan, whose self-critical stewardship of the Catholic Church's Truth, Justice and Healing Council has been the only redemption of an institution built on the preaching of forgiveness.

"I think it would have been a real sign of solidarity with the victims if we'd had some members of the hierarchy and senior figures from the church here," Sullivan said afterwards. "One can only assume they didn't fveel comfortable coming here."

The absence is terrible and unsurprising. The recurrent theme in five years of testimony at this commission has been abandonment. It is an abandonment of children and of responsibility.

The Royal Commission into Institutional Responses to Child Sexual Abuse investigated more than 4000 institutions. There were tens of thousands of victims. The 21-volume report from the commission was delivered to the governor-general on Friday.

The commission's chair, Justice Peter McClellan, confirmed the greatest number of abusers were hidden in Catholic institutions. This surprised no one. In hearing after hearing, an image emerged of an organisation that not only housed but enabled abuse. Paedophiles were shielded. Victims were disbelieved. Elaborate legal structures were built to deny rights.

When the commission was announced, George Pell's mind was fevered with conspiracy. He fumed and preened and blamed the press for a "persistent campaign" against the Catholic Church. He insisted Catholics were not the "only cab on the rank". Later, on the stand, he compared the church's culpability to a trucking company whose driver "picks up some lady and then molests her".

The commission's final report is an extraordinary document, extraordinary for the fact it exists. A redress scheme must now be set up. The thousands of lives hurt by institutional deviancy must not be left without repair. Other changes must be made and are among the recommendations.

But there is one larger change that must also take place. It is not called for in the official documents, but it is urgent and necessary. The church must no longer be allowed to interfere with public life.

In the course of this commission, the church has shown itself to disregard ordinary laws. Frequently, it operated in conflict with them. At the same time, it attempted to control the moral life of the country.

The church maintains undue influence over laws governing euthanasia and abortion and stem-cell research. It collects undue privilege from the tax system and for its shadow systems of education and healthcare. It holds obscene rights to discriminate against minorities. All of this must change.

Politics kowtows to faith, even as faith plays a diminished role in life. As church pews have emptied, the corridors of power have filled with lobbying priests and other defenders of clerical privilege. But this commission proves what has always been true: the church has no claim to superiority and no right to dictate to others. That lesson must be learnt. Our country would be better for it.

The Catholic Church was absent at the final hearing. It was never there for the children it abused, and this last day was no different. Malcolm Turnbull was present, though. He left through a side door.

Brutal force

The first punch lands after he is on the ground. His body is obscured by the men on top of him, but it appears to connect with the back of his head. The punches come in a flurry now, too many to count. There is a pause and then the police officer starts again. He changes arms. He stands so he can kick the man in the face.

Handcuffs are fitted. The man is black and shirtless. The officer takes a tool from his belt and uses it to bludgeon the man's head. He fits the tool back to his belt, without looking, as if this is normal. The camera catches him smiling. Standing again, he stomps on the man's head.

Later, the man kicks at him. The police officer throws him to the ground, kneels on his chest, and starts choking him. He lifts the man's body then drops it, his victim's head cracking against the floor.

Community lawyers have begun encouraging people to share footage such as this on social media. They don't trust the police to investigate themselves.

"A complaint system dealing with police brutality needs to be sufficiently robust and able to withstand scrutiny and you can't say that about the way the current police accountability mechanisms work," says Denis Nelthorpe, the chief executive at West Justice in Werribee, a district in outer Melbourne.

"People are being forced to find other ways to hold the powerful to account and one way to do that with great impact is to share footage in the community and let them judge that accordingly."

Other footage emerged this week, of a disability pensioner being beaten on the ground by six police officers. They used batons on his legs and back, fired pepper spray into his eyes. "You like that?" one of them taunts. "Smells good, doesn't it?"

Once handcuffed, the man is sprayed in the face with a hose. One of the police officers takes out a phone camera and his colleague performs for it, spraying the man again. They had been called to check his mental health.

"Our officers make mistakes like anyone else," a statement from Victoria Police said. "And when that happens, we seek to learn from them."

There are calls now for a royal commission. One should be held. The apparent ordinariness of this violence is an indictment on police.

This is the violence of a force whose own head of professional standards mourns the abolition of the lash. "The jigaboo runs riot and out of control," then assistant commissioner Brett Guerin wrote online, before resigning in disgrace last month. "The 'boo needs the lash. The 'boo wants the lash. Deep, deep down the 'boo knows the lash provides the governance and stability."

This is the violence of a force urged on by Peter Dutton and the Murdoch press, by an ex-cop and an amoral organisation. It is the violence of a force whose work has been politicised by the confection of a race crisis.

This is the violence of a force detached from reality – the detachment that imagines a city scared to go to dinner, as Dutton says Melbourne is, or overrun by gangs, as the Murdoch tabloids claim.

In both sets of footage, it is the smiles of the officers that are most terrifying. They are the smiles of people who know they will not be challenged, who know that the politics of this country encourages their excesses.

Nelson's new column

For a time the Australian War Memorial had trouble with children defecating in the decommissioned toilet of one of its naval exhibits. The metaphor is simple and apt.

This week, Brendan Nelson proposed that the war memorial be used to commemorate military involvement in Australia's campaign against asylum seekers – a war fought against innocent people. This solemn monument to loss in battle would be repurposed to honour the worst of our contemporary human rights abuses.

In an Anzac Day interview, Nelson said border protection was, "arguably the most important thing our military is doing with other agencies".

He said he spent two days on a patrol boat when he was defence minister in the Howard government and that he was struck by the courage of the young sailors. "If you ask the average Australian, out of all the things the Royal Australian Navy is doing, I'm pretty confident most would rank what these young men and women are doing in these patrol boats as pretty close to the top."

The politics of this gesture were clear. *The Australian* described it as a memorial for the "sailors who stopped illegal boat arrivals from landing here". Richard Marles broke ranks in the Labor Party to endorse it. Jim Molan, the co-architect of Operation Sovereign Borders, now a Liberal senator, said: "It is a legitimate part of Australian military history."

Finally, the militarisation of our immigration policy is complete. The public servants are in uniform. The policy is increasingly hostile and warlike. And the war memorial, that monument to blood and carnage, is waiting anxiously to commemorate the campaign.

"It is not something that will be done tomorrow, but some point in the future, all of those men and women who served in the border protection operations quite rightly would expect their story is going to be told at the Australian War Memorial," Nelson said. "If we do not invevst in more space soon, a decade or 20 years from now those veterans will be told, 'Look, I'm sorry, we can't tell your story ... because the war memorial doesn't have any space.'"

Here is the hustle in Nelson's pitch. The former Labor Party member, who once lied that he had never voted Liberal, is looking for $500 million to expand the war memorial. He knows that there is no limit to what governments will spend on the demonisation of refugees, and so he is chasing that cruel money.

The navy loathes turnbacks. They are dangerous and traumatic. There is no doubt that this work is difficult and that it is forced on service people by our politics. But it is still worth asking what Nelson's memorial would commemorate.

Would it commemorate the camps these people are pushed into once they have been intercepted? Would it commemorate the torturous conditions? The mental degradation? The murder by guards? The suicides and immolations? The rapes? The soliciting in detention of women for sex?

Nelson's proposal is an opportunistic one. That is fitting: the whole system of offshore detention is opportunistic. It's a system built not for refugees but for swinging voters, a system of gross imperfection, of cruelties and incompetence. There is no plan for it, nothing beyond votes. That is how these men and women have ended up marooned, with no clear prospects. That is how these lives have been ruined.

It is hard to know how a system so flawed, so broken, might be commemorated. It is worrying to think it might be glorified. But that, it seems, is what is happening.

The fact of murder

In the flats where she lived, she would always jump the bottom step. The neighbours would hear it, the pause and then the thud of her platform shoes.

She was "very intelligent", a neighbour told *The Age*. "She kept to herself. She was very much an introvert."

Her name was Eurydice Dixon. Some friends called her Ridi. Near midnight on Tuesday, she sent a message to a friend: "I'm almost home safe." Somewhere in the next few hours, she was killed.

Dixon was a stand-up comic. She was 22. She was walking home from a gig when she was murdered.

"She was on top of the world because her gig went so well," a friend said.

Dixon was breaking through. Her last festival show played to full rooms.

"I couldn't get my head around how she could stand on stage even when the crowd didn't get her humour. It didn't shake her, she could stand tall against that," a colleague told *The Age*.

"You just don't get sensibility like that in someone so young because at 22 years old most don't have enough to say, but she did.

"She had life experience, she was mature beyond her years and that's the tragedy of all this."

Other comics called her "an important and funny voice". The venue where she often played said she was a "remarkable, talented, kind, unique and universally loved person".

On Thursday, a 19-year-old man was charged with her rape and murder. He handed himself in on Wednesday night. He did not apply for bail.

Police offered their crude boilerplate, told people to protect themselves: "The message we would provide to all members of the community is to take responsibility for your safety."

And: "This is an area of high community activity ... so just make sure you have situational awareness, that you're aware of your surroundings."

And: "Make sure people know where you are and that if you've got a mobile phone, carry it. And if you've got any concerns, call police."

We must reckon with a society that is not safe. It is a society of violence and entitlement. Our institutions have not the language or the tools to begin dismantling this.

Eurydice Dixon was murdered because someone felt entitled to kill her. The horrifying randomness of the crime makes it news, but it does not change that basic fact. Society has to change the basic fact.

Counting the dead

Margaret Indich (38)
Antonia Tatchell (43)
Amelia Blake (22)
Nancy Barclay (83)
Nowra Khatib (61)
Unnamed woman (41)
Radmila Stevanovic (65)
Sally Rothe (54)
Le Ngoc Le (77)
Marija Karovska (51)
Unnamed woman (20)
Kerrie Keath (68)
Katherine Daley (29)
Simone Fraser (57)
Unnamed woman (59)
Teah Luckwell (22)
Kay Dix (71)
Unnamed woman (62)
Cecilia Haddad (38)
Unnamed woman (46)
Debbie Combarngo (37)
Katrina Miles (35)
Cynda Miles (58)
Karen Ashcroft (52)
Unnamed woman (37)
Unnamed woman (46)
Caroline Willis (69)
Unnamed woman (69)
Qi Yu (28)
Eurydice Dixon (22)

Research by Destroy The Joint and Counting Dead Women
Australia. Known deaths due to violence against women in
Australia in 2018.

Razing a Voice

Mick Dodson says it was a door slammed. He says Malcolm Turnbull's response to the Uluru Statement from the Heart was "deplorable".

Speaking at the National Press Club this week, he said Turnbull was guilty of "a gross distortion of what was said at Uluru and it's shameful that it's come from the head of the country, the person elected to lead the country".

This distortion was done by press release. The greatest consensus ever reached in Indigenous politics was dismissed by email.

The voice to the parliament was formally mischaracterised. Turnbull made clear he would not argue for it and would not address misapprehension of it. He rejected the proposal not for what it was but how it might be seen. "It would," he said, without irony or clear attribution, "inevitably become seen as a third chamber of parliament."

Noel Pearson answered this speciousness with angry truth. "Turnbull, as prime minister, has chosen to lie about his prior knowledge of the proposal for an Indigenous voice, and indeed his endorsement of it as sensible more than two years before he rejected it …" he wrote in *The Monthly*.

"Turnbull supported the Indigenous voice to parliament when he was not prime minister, but then ended up calling it a 'third chamber of parliament' when he was, knowing full well that was a gross untruth.

"He did this because he was trapped by his political situation: devoid of capital, hostage to the conservatives whose leader he had stabbed in order to gain the prime ministership, and without the gumption to break his captivity."

It is much easier to think of failings in Turnbull's prime ministership than it is to think of successes. Even so, his condescending dismissal of the Uluru statement numbers among his worst. It will be remembered as the shame of his leadership.

It is through cynicism and lack of imagination that he ignores the voice of First Australians. He is content with their absence from formal recognition in the processes of our parliament. He has failed them and in doing so he has failed this country.

Earlier this week, Pat Dodson said First Nations people were willing to take a "pragmatic" approach to recognition. "The question of the permanency or guarantee of a voice in the constitution is a nice idea but it's very difficult to see how you would be guaranteed an opportunity to have a say on legislation and policies at every point," he said. "It's still under investigation."

Pat Dodson is working with Liberal MP Julian Leeser on proposals for recognition. It is worthy work, though slow and complicated.

It wouldn't be happening if Turnbull had a willingness to believe in the country he is supposed to govern, if he had allowed the public a vote on the voice.

That vote would have carried, and Australia would be more whole for it.

Bad eggs and Latham

It is hard to imagine a better illustration of the slow, bleak decline of our politics than the roboticised voice of Mark Latham imploring voters to elect One Nation.

The former leader of the Labor Party, a protégé of Gough Whitlam's, the man who wrote *Civilising Global Capital*, is shilling for a party of racists and cranks. Here we are at the ugly, arm-breaking end of the taxi ride that has been his time in public life. Here is Mark, flushed-faced and sweating, arguing over the fare.

Latham says he recorded a second message, this time for the Liberal Democrats, a party to which he also has membership. Here lies this country's one-time preferred prime minister. Here lies the dignity of our sad, broken politics.

In Longman, where the Latham calls are playing, One Nation has preferenced Jim Saleam ahead of Labor. For those who don't remember, Saleam spent the 1980s wearing a swastika on his arm. He went to prison for his role in a shotgun attack on a representative of the African National Congress. As Latham's recording says: "Please support minor parties and independents to shake up the system and put some honest politics back into Canberra."

Latham is tragedy and farce in a single body. On Sky News he and Graham Richardson scream defamations at each other, two crows hopping and squabbling over a carcass. Here is the sustaining shame of this country, the culture of rewarded failure that sees these relics still shaping what we are. A man with no morals argues against a man with no brain. It has the quality of a sideshow amusement. It is also our democracy.

The jokes were never funny and now they have come to life. Peta Credlin sits down to write a book titled *On Character*. Her publisher asks if "the idea of a person of good character disappeared in the era of personality politics".

At time of writing, promotional material for the book had been removed from the publisher's website. Perhaps out of shame. In Australian politics, this is not thought of as ironic. Australian politics doesn't have the subtlety for irony. You promise character and then you take it away and it just is.

The same publisher gave this country *The Latham Diaries* and Tony Abbott's *Battlelines* manifesto and a working substitute for intellectual life. We are drowning in a soup bowl of ideas.

On Twitter he is "Real Mark Latham", as if the rest of the time it was an act. Unmasked, he is a Rivers catalogue of cruel misogyny and transphobic venom, a man who wears wraparound sunglasses and believes brown is colourful. He mocks schoolchildren and working mothers, disbelieves psychiatry and demands that everyone speak English.

Mark Latham is a gout on our politics. But the whole Falstaffian body is set with pox. It is a picture of sad urges and failing organs. Its ills trace back to men such as Mark, to the basement out of which he now broadcasts, but they do not end there.

Watching as children were freed from a cave in Thailand, the capacity of the human spirit for good flickered and lit. The editor of this country's premier journal of conservative thought disagreed, however. "It wasn't a bunch of gender-fluid divers that went down there," Rowan Dean said. "It wasn't a bunch of touchy-feely identity politics, diverse and inclusive, unconscious bias mob who saved those boys' lives. It was solid Western know-how and technology."

Sometimes it really feels as if all the world's ills can be traced back to middle-aged men clinging desperately to their relevance, men whose anxieties about equality smother all else. These men are busy placing robocalls from the graves of their careers.

Gang of fear

Christopher Pyne doesn't understand the question. That's the point of a dog whistle: not everyone can hear it.

A journalist asks if he is afraid to go out to restaurants in Melbourne, and he looks confused. "No. Why?" He looks the other way, laughs. "Should I be?"

The journalist explains that the prime minister has repeated this claim, first made by Peter Dutton, that people fear going out to dinner in Victoria. "Oh," Pyne remembers, joining in the alternative reality where this is true. "Because of the gangs, the violence. I'm sorry, I wasn't following you … I didn't understand the question."

Pyne is this government's willingness. He has a schoolboy's desire to please. As soon as he was reminded of the act, he was eager to play along. The smile never left his face.

On Thursday, Dutton joined in again. "It's like some parallel universe going on down there at the moment where you're not allowed to refer to these people as 'in gangs'," he said. "I mean, it's fairyland stuff."

Dutton freights in a kind of mock indignation – in sarcasm, the lowest form of politics. "I'm a racist, and there's been a 70 per cent spike in the number of complaints to the Human Rights Commissioner in Victoria because I called people involved in home invasions 'African gang members', even though they're of African descent and they're involved in gang activity in Victoria."

Malcolm Turnbull indulges this. He pretends the rule of law has broken down in Victoria. He talks the same fiction as the pamphlets his party is stuffing into letterboxes, with photo library youths and warnings of gangs in hunting packs. The same pamphlets ignore the drop in crime, the absence of evidence that Sudanese migrants are over-represented among offenders.

"There is concern about the state government's failure to uphold the rule of law on the streets," Turnbull says. "There is a real concern about that."

And again: "The fact is there is a gang issue here and you are not going to make it go away by pretending it doesn't exist. At some point you have to be fair dinkum and you have to acknowledge that there is a concern, people are concerned about it."

And again: "I have heard people, colleagues from Melbourne, say that there is real anxiety about crime in Melbourne. There is real concern about street crime. There is real concern about Sudanese gangs."

And again: "It is critically important that people are not afraid to go out and not afraid to walk the streets and it is important that the police have the full backing of a government."

This is the pantomime to which Christopher Pyne was being understudied. He was laughing because it was so ludicrous. The prime minister would claim for the sake of a few byelections and the Victorian Opposition that the second most populous state in this country is without the rule of law. He would claim that Sudanese gangs roam the streets, that people are fearful to leave their homes, that the police have lost the support of government and control of the cities.

Christopher Pyne might laugh, incredulous and aloof, but this joke is a serious one. This little, scripted farce is about the oppression of a single minority; it is about the politics of division and the effectiveness of racism in maintaining anxiety. It is about the eagerness of our politicians to lie for votes.

Peter Dutton is right about one thing. He is a racist. That's the problem with sarcasm: if you are already lying, it's hard to burlesque the bit you want people to believe as true.

Fairfax to middling

When Fairfax moved its Sydney papers to a purpose-built office in Pyrmont, the joke was that the building resembled the H-block prison designed to extinguish hope in IRA fighters. That was a decade ago.

The building now belongs to Google. The internet giant leased floor after floor until, in January, it consumed the entire premises. Desk by desk, it was as if the search engine was doing in reality what it was doing online. The lease Fairfax initially signed was supposed to run until 2027. The last journalist will be out the year after next.

As of Thursday, it was not just the building. The papers are gone, too. They will soon belong to Nine. The story of Fairfax under Greg Hywood looks more and more like the story of Maze prison. Journalists have been on the blanket since before he took over. He will be remembered as the warder who watched Bobby Sands die.

Fairfax describes the move as a merger, but in reality it has been bought. Nine's chief executive will remain chief executive. The name of the business will be Nine. Hywood will take a generous exit package.

It is too soon to say what the broadcaster wants from the metropolitan papers, from *The Sydney Morning Herald*, *The Age* and *The Australian Financial Review*. In the past, it has expressed ambivalence. Already, it is talking about unwanted duplication.

The local papers will possibly be sold. More redundancies can be expected. The real interest is in the streaming service Stan and the real estate website Domain. Fairfax's storied journalism, the more than 170 years of faith stored in its mastheads, is mostly an inconvenience.

This has been inevitable since, with the help of One Nation, the government dissolved the country's media ownership laws. The communications minister, who used to work for Peter Costello, will now watch as his old boss becomes chair of a company that further concentrates our already concentrated media.

Paul Keating calls the deal "an exceptionally bad development". He said Nine will inevitably run the editorial policy of the papers it has bought, and that it has shown no ethical or moral capacity to do so.

"No one has lanced the carbuncle at the centre of Nine's approach to news management. And, as sure as night follows day, that pus will inevitably leak into Fairfax," he said. "For the country, this is a great pity."

Journalism depends on diversity. It is too expensive a craft for a single company to do it alone. This merger imperils hundreds of jobs. It also weakens our democracy.

Very little will stop this deal. In one way or another, the damage done to Fairfax is a byproduct of One Nation's desperate attempts to wound the ABC. Our media is in terrible strife. The government is untroubled by this. Indeed, it has encouraged it.

The reason for this is simple: the less the public knows, the better it is for politicians.

In the early 1990s, Malcolm Turnbull acted with Kerry Packer in a covert takeover bid for Fairfax. Turnbull leaked Packer's involvement in the consortium and the Nine boss was thrown out of the deal. Turnbull said Packer's involvement was "not only stupid but contrary to everyone's interests".

In leaking the details, Turnbull put himself at risk. Packer threatened to have him killed. Turnbull believed this threat to be credible, but he acted on principle. That was before he was prime minister.

On Barnaby Joyce

Barnaby Joyce says it is like a boarding school. The corollary is that he must think of himself as a child.

"If you become part of that boarding school, then you will try to make that your life and you will try to get ahead in that boarding school called Parliament House," he said this week. "Big, white building on top of a hill. It's a boarding school because you all travel down there. They ring the bell, you go here. They ring the bell, you go there. You all eat dinner together. Sometimes, you sleep together."

That is the problem with Joyce: the politics never elevates above the schoolyard. He is a child and he is indulged by a system built for childish men. The bell he complains of is the one that asks him to vote on legislations, the one that encourages him to do his job. Urges call to him but duty is not one of them.

Politics as Joyce describes it is without responsibility. As he made his way between television interviews this week, selling his unctuous memoir, he presented himself as a man to whom life simply happened.

He described himself straying in bars, depressed, medicating with alcohol. He described himself as a lie.

"Winston Churchill had his black dog: mine was a half-crazed cattle dog, biting everything that came near the yard," he writes in his book.

"But the downside comes as well, when you get sad in the afternoon because it's the afternoon and there are not enough clouds in the sky ..."

Mental illness is an issue that bedevils high office. Joyce is right to reflect on the demands of public life, on the peculiar strains of our democracy. He is right to call it isolating.

But for Joyce, these concerns are not systemic. His worry is for himself. He is bitter at his treatment, still smarting at the outcome of his affair. His anger at Malcolm Turnbull is petty and misplaced, his position as untenable now as it was then.

Joyce is and was a study in self-interest. It defined his portfolios, emboldened his hypocrisy. He is a vision of entitlement. His whole life has been a boarding school, an edifice to uninterrogated privilege.

To watch Joyce this week was to watch a man who once held the second highest office in the country parading between radio spots as if he were a contestant evicted from a reality TV show. There was the same vacuity, the same grasping opportunism.

There was a sense in this one man of everything our politics lacks, not because it was there in him but because it was so conspicuously absent and because that absence has never once held him back.

"The proceeds of the book go to me," he said in one interview, growing slightly defensive. "And to, um, to support my family. And that's about it. And if I can ... remember, I'm basically supporting two families at the moment."

Joyce is making do, as the country has since he entered politics.

Enter the void

Australia rests gently on the precipice of farce. It has done so for some time.

Our democracy never recovered from Kevin Rudd's second, brief stint as prime minister. In those two months, the office became a triumph of venality.

When Rudd lost the leadership to Julia Gillard three years earlier, he did so because he was unable to continue governing. His office was in chaos. The flaws in his character were tearing apart his government.

When he challenged Gillard in 2012, unsuccessfully, he did so for no reason but self-interest. When he challenged again in 2013, that self-interest aligned with the party's. Nowhere was there concern for the nation or the office or the people he was supposed to represent.

In the politics that has followed, the one constant has been instability. The policy achievements of the past five years have been negligible. It has proved impossible to govern in this broken system.

Then, as now, the mess is helped along by a bored and restless media, made cynical by its loss of power and emboldened by old structures that haven't noticed it is gone. Witless figures such as Ray Hadley thrill at the thought of influence, and aged ones such as Alan Jones glory at the thought of revenge. As is tradition, the tabloids sell out their readers to the status quo.

On Thursday, Malcolm Turnbull said Australians were "rightly appalled by what they're witnessing in their nation's parliament today and in the course of this week". He described a campaign to "bully and intimidate" parliamentary colleagues and "pull the party further to the right". He described the situation as a "madness".

All this is true, and all of it his fault. He is no better than the parliament he is in. Nor is Bill Shorten. Both are beneficiaries of the same hungry-handed avarice, the same opportunism and disregard, the same plotting and counterplotting, the same hubris and lost purpose.

Meanwhile, a child sets herself alight on Nauru, trapped in a system this parliament built. The country coasts towards oblivion with no credible policy on climate change. The public school system atrophies. The health system struggles on, underfunded.

A reckoning is coming, but not of the kind we have seen this week. An election will not fix this, either. The whole system of preselection is broken and it has given us the parliament of hucksters and also-rans through which we now suffer.

It is not that the system fails to attract talent; it is that it seems to preclude it. If anything is to change, people from outside the machine need to run for parliament. People reading this need to run for parliament, people without patronage or preening expectation.

People need to stand not out of self-interest but out of concern for the country in which they live. Our politics can no longer survive its own emptiness. It has created a vacuum, a kind of two-party void.

Perhaps it is true that a nation gets the government it deserves. But surely no nation deserves this.

Scott (2018–2022)

Winning ugly

It makes sense once you appreciate that this is no longer about governing. The one constant in politics – holding power – has been cast aside. With it go the orthodoxies of logic and reason.

This is about ideology. This is about giving up on the country, on what it wants, because a stubborn few cannot give up on coal and traditional values. The Coalition would sooner forsake electoral success than reckon with the realities of climate science or engage with the leadership asked for by multiculturalism.

Scott Morrison is prime minister not because he has a better chance than Malcolm Turnbull of winning the next election. He is prime minister because he is more willing to govern against the desires of the electorate.

There are little concessions. There is rugby league on the television in the prime minister's office. There is a signed football and a model aeroplane, the promise of his polo-shirted ordinariness. "If we win today," he says to his treasurer, cameras spluttering, "we'll go into the top four."

There is the Australian flag pin he fixes to his lapel, like a travel agent or an accountant at a conference overseas. He has given one to each of his ministers.

"I've been wearing this now for many, many years. I can't remember when I started doing this," he said at their first cabinet meeting.

"The reason I wear it is because it reminds me every single day whose side I'm on. I'm on the side of the Australian people, that's what I'm saying to myself, that's who I think about first."

These are small gestures, the politics of Lilliput. They are a sop to an imagined base. But the Liberal Party can't be serious if it thinks this is about the electorate, that replacing their most popular figure with a man who couldn't sell a budget was about any kind of future.

The circus rolls on. Tony Abbott is given a position as special envoy on Indigenous affairs, as if it is a lucky door prize. Peter Dutton gives humanitarian aid to a string of au pairs. It is 1950 again and the two biggest issues in the country are drought and electricity prices.

The polls are sceptical. Of course they are. The calamity of the past fortnight was never about votes. Better the party decide what it is not than stumble forward into what it might be.

Imagination is a scarce resource in politics. As is the twin quality of hopefulness. Morrison had long imagined himself prime minister, but his party spent no time in imagining what sort of country he would lead. And so we are here.

Morrison's team, the Cronulla Sharks, beat the Newcastle Knights on Sunday. No doubt, he is keen to succeed as prime minister. But the party that destroyed his predecessor has no credible plan for his own tenure. It is unlikely there is any intention of making one, either. This was never about winning, and so the country loses.

Gender trouble

Scott Morrison governs in the assured first person. His curiosity ends at the limits of his own experience. He speaks as a man whose imagination reaches as far as Kurnell. Like John Howard, he believes leading the country is the same as organising a barbecue.

He speaks "as a parent". For complex questions, he forms a quorum: "Jenny and I." He defers to his faith. He rules in his own image.

Morrison is untroubled by gay conversion therapy. He has the luxury of not caring. "I respect people of all sexualities," he says, and then, as if the two things are even, as if one does not embolden the abuse of the other: "I respect people of all religions, all faiths."

He won't be drawn on recommendations to ban the practice, on the advice of doctors or the evidence of barbarism. "I've never been involved in anything like that, I've never supported anything like that," he says, as if the question is of him and not his office. "It's just not an issue for me and I'm not planning to get engaged in the issue."

Scott Morrison forgets something because likely it should never have been true: he is prime minister. The questions he answers are no longer hypothetical. He no longer decides whether he is engaged. This is his job. It is a job he does not understand.

"We do not need 'gender whisperers' in our schools," he writes on social media, sharing a vile, distorted piece from *The Daily Telegraph*. "Let kids be kids."

This is the other lesson from Howard's barbecue prime ministership: if you are to reach outside your experience, let it only be to stoke fears and misrepresent facts. Let it only be to demonise an other.

Morrison condemns the teaching of sexual diversity in schools. He panics at the idea of support for trans and non-binary children. Alone among prime ministers, he says he abandoned public education because of the values taught in it. "It's not happening in the school I send my kids to, and that's one of the reasons I send them there."

Simona Castricum is a musician, a trans woman and PhD candidate in architecture at the University of Melbourne. The morning of Scott Morrison's "gender whisperers" comments, she was twice abused by men from their cars.

"There's often a spike in harassment towards the transgender community at the times when our leaders and media pundits single us out with hate speech," she wrote afterwards. "It gives permission for people to think their prejudiced ideas are justifiable beliefs that need to be shouted from cars or in playgrounds. It's the Australian way – passed down through the generations – with transphobia a staple in the diet of the bully."

No doubt this is not an issue for Morrison. He has never been involved with anything like that. He's probably not planning to get engaged in it.

Perhaps that is okay for Morrison, but it is not okay for a prime minister. No longer are his thoughts an expression of his limits: they are an image for the country. On the evidence of this week, it is a narrow and scared one, unconcerned for the rights of others, indifferent to minorities, willing to stake its comfort on the suffering of trans children. Here we are in a new, worse Australia, and it's only been a fortnight.

News agency

It's not just the *Herald Sun*. It's a media that is fragile and defensive, built on unquestioned values. It's the uncomfortable realisation that we can be wrong – that the ethics we hold dear as journalists were honed in rooms of men, drawn from the same class, the same race, the same schools. These values didn't change even as the newsrooms changed, and the newsrooms didn't change enough. And now, in an age of insecurity, we rely on a confidence that was based on unchecked privilege – and we are mostly too scared to check it further.

Newspapers are built on an expectation of truthfulness. They are embarrassed by their errors, undermined by their fallibility. Largely, this has served them well. It has created a culture of earnestness and accuracy. It has also made journalists protective – unwilling to challenge the assumptions of their craft, lest their whole purpose crumble.

A cub reporter knocks on the door of a grieving woman for the simple reason that cub reporters have always knocked on the doors of grieving women. This intrusion is uncritical and unremarkable, its purpose lost somewhere between the spot that waits for the story and the audience there to read it. Infrequently do we worry about the woman. Some of us will say she wanted to tell her story. Journalism is like nature: it's what we've always done.

It is not surprising the *Herald Sun* cannot hear criticism about Mark Knight's depiction of Serena Williams. For them, the matter is uncomplicated: "Mark Knight cartoon not racist or sexist."

They maintain that racism is a question of intent. They believe an act can be stripped of its context and an image denuded of its history. They feel the authority to make these assertions for the simple reason that they have always had it. They are not impeded by their own whiteness in this task; they are emboldened by it.

The Murdoch press is a caricature of racist provincialism. They publish Andrew Bolt and sanctify Bill Leak. But the rest of the media suffers many of the same issues. We struggle to hear criticism. We deify our work. We fluctuate between victimhood and privilege, unable to reconcile our power with our lessening means, keen to defend what it is we do, the great social import of this work, and yet in doing so overlook the occasions on which we transgress.

Earlier this year, *National Geographic* conducted an inquiry into its own racial biases. It commissioned University of Virginia professor John Edwin Mason to lead the process. The editorial announcing the issue was blunt: "For decades, our coverage was racist. To rise above our past, we must acknowledge it."

Mason found a magazine alive with cliché and condescension. He found views that reflected their time and did nothing to lead readers beyond it.

"Americans got ideas about the world from Tarzan movies and crude racist caricatures," he said afterwards. "Segregation was the way it was. *National Geographic* wasn't teaching as much as reinforcing messages they already received and doing so in a magazine that had tremendous authority. *National Geographic* comes into existence at the height of colonialism, and the world was divided into the colonisers and the colonised. That was a colour line, and *National Geographic* was reflecting that view of the world."

The media as a whole – *The Saturday Paper* included – could benefit from similar work in this country. It need not be historic, unfortunately. There is enough in this past fortnight to fill a newspaper with apologies.

Until we do this work, we will continue to report from the past and find ourselves in conflict with the realities of our present. Looking across at this week, we are no longer the first draft of history: we are its unsold reprints.

We need greater diversity. We need greater curiosity about our purpose. We need a willingness to confront the fact that we can be wrong and that we are. There is no use pretending this is limited to the more grotesque excesses of our craft: it is present in the unrepresentative everyday of our entire industry. We ask questions of everyone but ourselves.

Fair bunkum

The problem with Scott Morrison is that it seems as if he is pretending. When he looks up from his phone screen to address the camera in his office, he has all the credibility of a corporate training video. He is avuncular and insincere, and then he starts to speak.

"We've got to get electricity prices down," he says, rushing. "I met Avril and Colin this morning. Colin served in our defence forces and is a defence force pensioner. Avril's gone back to work to pay for the bills."

The details of this story have as much to do with the policy Morrison is announcing as the policy has to do with addressing climate change. This doesn't matter.

Morrison holds up a sheet of paper. "This is their electricity bill. You can see it's paid, but they are paying too much."

You can see neither of these things.

"I look through your comments and you say, 'Well, how you going to do it?'" Morrison says, his face folding with concern: "We're going to get the electricity companies in line. We're going to do it with new laws and new rules, which means they can't rip you off simply by you being a loyal customer. If you stay with them you shouldn't be penalised for that. We're going to stop the price gouging and have tough penalties for the big electricity companies if they try and do that. And thirdly, we're going to force them to put more fair dinkum, reliable energy, power, into the system."

Morrison goes on like this, rocking forward in his chair, his jacket off to show he is working hard. There is satisfaction in the phrase "fair dinkum" – his ocker euphemism for coal.

The condescension in this video is not just to the Avrils and Colins who people Morrison's Australia, whose bills and service records he uses as props. The condescension is to climate change and to energy policy.

The price control is a fiddle: some bills will go down, others will go up. The cost to the environment is the cost of a country with no policy on climate change, willing to destroy the Earth for politics.

"Renewables are great," Morrison says, his expression unchanged, as if calibrating a polygraph. "But we're also needing the reliable power when the sun isn't shining and the wind isn't blowing. That's what keeps the lights on. Lower electricity prices. Meeting our emissions reductions targets. And ensuring the lights stay on."

Morrison says all this in a phantasm of ordinariness. He keeps a picture of the Queen in his office and one of each of his children. A statue depicts two soldiers in the act of mateship. On his bookshelf are spy novels, a few popular histories, Nam Le's collection *The Boat*, and, apparently, no room for irony.

Morrison's Australia is aggressively pedestrian. It prefers to be wrong than complex. It values work over ingenuity, rejects the world because it is anxious about its place in it.

That's what is most worrying about these videos Morrison makes. They re-create the worst version of Australia: prideful and insecure, too afraid to act on anything more than what it already knows.

There is no plan in this country to address climate change. We are going backwards. Scott Morrison is there, waiting for us. He's set up a camera and taken off his jacket and is pretending to look at his phone.

The dark room

The story begins with a horse race, with boys and girls, pulling at their restive charges, naked in the morning air. The course is marked by banners, which flutter and snap in the breeze. Everything is cheer and sweetness. There is joy even in the clatter of bells.

The writer doesn't trouble for specifics. She is happy for the reader to decide. Perhaps this is a city of subway trains and floating lights and fuel-free power. Perhaps not. Perhaps here the common cold has been cured, or it hasn't.

Ursula K. Le Guin says that some things are certain in this city, which she calls Omelas. The author says there is no guilt. She says the people who live here are singularly happy – happy above all else – but that does not make them simple.

She says, if you wish, to imagine a fairytale or an orgy. She says to imagine nakedness and tambourines and beloved children. There are no clergy and no soldiers. Contentedness is generous and the sense of triumph magnanimous.

There is music and food. Le Guin describes both in detail – a guide, should it help the reader to imagine. She does not know the laws of this society but she suspects there are few.

In the basement of an opulent public building, or perhaps under a private manor, there is a room with one locked door and no window. The light is second-hand, spilling between cracks. The floor is dirt and mop heads stand stiff in a bucket. The room is no larger than a closet.

"In the room a child is sitting," Le Guin writes. "It could be a boy or a girl. It looks about six, but actually is nearly ten."

The child is enfeebled by abuse. It fears the mops. Occasionally its door rattles and a person is there or several people and they beat the child. Others look with disgusted eyes. The child speaks less and less. Its body is withered with malnutrition. There are sores where it has sat in excrement.

"They all know it is there, all the people of Omelas," Le Guin writes. "Some of them have come to see it, others are content merely to know it is there. They all know that it has to be there. Some of them understand why, and some do not, but they all understand that their happiness, the beauty of their city, the tenderness of their friendships, the health of their children, the wisdom of their scholars, the skill of their makers, even the abundance of their harvest and the kindly weathers of their skies, depend wholly on this child's abominable misery."

Le Guin writes that this is explained to children in Omelas when they are between eight and 12. She says it is mostly the young who want to see the child and that whenever they do, no matter how prepared, they feel revulsion and impotence.

"But there is nothing they can do," she writes. "If the child were brought up into the sunlight out of that vile place, if it were cleaned and fed and comforted, that would be a good thing indeed; but if it were done, in that day and hour all the prosperity and beauty and delight of Omelas would wither and be destroyed. Those are the terms. To exchange all the goodness and grace of every life in Omelas for that single, small improvement: to throw away the happiness of thousands for the chance of the happiness of one: that would be to let guilt within the walls indeed. The terms are strict and absolute; there may not even be a kind word spoken to the child."

When this story was published in 1973, it was as a thought experiment. The idea of perpetual suffering, forced on a child for the benefit of an otherwise benign society, of endless detention and terrible deprivation, was science fiction.

And yet here we are. Even as the children are slowly pulled from Nauru, Peter Dutton defends the Omelas he has built. He refuses to accept there are humanitarian reasons for closing the camps. He looks prideful at the damaged lives and warns that compassion is a pull factor. He says only that the bolted room with its clotted mops is too expensive to keep.

Le Guin's society is one without guilt. She imagined this would be necessary to sustain the horrors of her fiction, because she could not imagine Peter Dutton or a country that would, with all the faculties of its conscience, still accept such a compact.

The man who wasn't there

It is as if Scott Morrison is getting smaller. With each passing week, the member for Cook shrinks into his leadership.

His government has lost its majority. It intends hardly to sit next year. Its early budget seems to promise a May election, and on all accounts Morrison will likely lose it. His prime ministership is set to last no more than nine months.

Ordinarily, there is a moment in which a person becomes prime minister – a moment beyond the swearing in, when events transform a person into the office.

For John Howard, it was in the furnace of his gun reform. For Kevin Rudd, it was the gravity of the apology to the Stolen Generations. For Julia Gillard, it was myriad small acts that will cohere in popular memory around her royal commission into child abuse.

Tony Abbott never had his moment. He never experienced the alchemy of circumstances and action that transmute a person into statesmanship. Likely, Malcolm Turnbull missed his. No bold actions, no signature policy. He points to marriage equality and hopes history will misrecord him as its architect.

Morrison, on current projections, will be remembered for sending an empty bus across Queensland. He is not looking for the moment that transforms him: he is looking down camera, squinting, in a hat Mick Fanning's mum gave him.

The Australia he communes with is an Australia of the past, a faded travel commercial about a country unafraid to be simple. It is as if he was never sacked at Tourism Australia and instead the country was winnowed down into its remit.

The longer Morrison tries at this, the more inauthentic he becomes. His signature has changed to trace out a nickname: Scomo. His language is overburdened with ingratiating ockerisms. His whole presence carries the anxiety of a man waiting to be found out.

Without that moment of transformation – even with it – the office tends to reveal the falseness of its holder. Gillard addressed it explicitly, announcing when her "real" self had arrived. Turnbull governed without his convictions and the polls consistently reminded him of this. Rudd mangled his way through ordinariness. You could see where the personality had been fitted to him, the seams in the latex stretched over the robot.

More and more, Morrison looks like a man without a purpose. He makes hollow appeals to race and the economy. He goads Labor with divisive cant: "Don't get me started on 50,000 illegal arrivals and blowing the Budget."

He stubbornly refuses the realities of climate change. When a progressive agenda is overwhelmingly endorsed in the Victorian election, he sends the returned premier a text message. He sees no lessons in it.

A fair criticism of Malcolm Turnbull was that he didn't stand for anything. The worrying reality for Scott Morrison is that he stands for even less.

Often, it seems as if he is holding his eyes closed – like he is counting in a game of hide and seek. It is not clear what he is seeking, or what is being hidden, but the announcement of next year's sitting calendar gets him closer to the point when he will have to open them.

It remains to be seen if anything will be different, or if he will ever become prime minister.

Knowing Brenton Tarrant

Perhaps the strangest response was Paul Maley's. The defence and national security editor at *The Australian* was at pains to make clear that the Christchurch terrorist did not read Australian news.

"Christchurch shooter Brenton Tarrant might have been born and bred in Grafton, but the ideology that inspired him came straight from ancient racisms of Europe and the fanaticism of medieval Christians," Maley wrote.

"With Australia's political class poised for a national bout of cultural self-loathing following Tarrant's Christchurch terror attack, it is worth noting there is zero evidence the man paid any attention to anything said or done in this country since 2014."

Maley stepped through the broad topics of Tarrant's manifesto: Emmanuel Macron's election in France, the NATO-led war on Kosovo, the birth rate in the Muslim community, the Siege of Vienna. "It's vile stuff," he wrote, "but nowhere does it mention Pauline Hanson, Operation Sovereign Borders, Sky After Dark or any of the other right-wing villains being fitted up as accessories before the fact. The word 'Australia' or 'Australian' appears just 11 times."

Maley doesn't deny Australia's Islamophobia, or the danger of stoking hatred and division. He just wants it to be known that Tarrant was radicalised by it somewhere else. It's like a gun shop owner saying someone bought the weapons next door.

Elsewhere in the same newspaper, Janet Albrechtsen wrote of the "political ratbags" who would "exploit cold-blooded terrorism by a white supremacist in New Zealand ozn Friday |for their narrow-minded, illiberal political agendas".

She warned against calls for laws to "penalise media outlets, and figures that consistently promote fear and hatred" and "robust laws against the spread of hate speech". She cautioned those who would "fall for claims that this censorship, under the ruse of clamping down on hate speech, will stamp out terrorism".

The risk she warns of is not to people but to ideology. She sees free speech as an argument against responsibility. Like many in the press, she refuses to acknowledge the role the media plays in radicalisation.

There is an urgent desire to blame internet forums for Tarrant's bent interpretation of the world. The bigger concern is that many of the thoughts expressed in his manifesto have appeared, in one form or another, on the opinion pages of most mainstream publications in this country.

Tarrant is an aberration, as is all terrorism. But he is produced by a culture that has normalised hate, that is built from division, whose politics routinely exploits fear and whose press caters enthusiastically to it.

The same politics says there are bad people on both sides. The press says the mass shooter was on holiday in Europe and probably missed their racist articles. What both are doing is maintaining the status quo, shifting culpability, minimising their actions.

The world gets no safer in a system such as this. The prime minister visits a mosque, then announces an immigration cut. The journalist prepares another piece on the rights of bigots. As the lawyer Nyadol Nyuon said this week: "You can't get to the heart of our stories, can't understand us, can't truly empathise, when your priority is free speech and ours is to live."

Nothing to see here

Scott Morrison has the appearance of a school principal in an enrolment video. He has a soft-focus vision for Australia, where children gambol on the lawn and somewhere, just to the right of camera, is a person in whom he wishes to confide an earnest truth.

"The real question is, is what country do you want to live in for the next 10 years?" he says. "The next 10 years is going to determine people's lives."

He blinks, as if to hold back emotion. He is grappling with the import of what he has to say. "Starting out, coming out of university. Having kids. Entering retirement. The next 10 years are important to everybody, at every stage of life. The decisions they'll make – if we get the settings right, on our economy and on security – if we create the right conditions then Australians will have a better next decade."

The words don't quite fit together. The longer the sentences become, the less they contain. "That the choices that my girls will have over the next 10 years, even over the next three years, will set up … see, the decisions you make in one term of government last for a decade or more. So it isn't just about the next three years; it's about what does the next decade look like?"

He is on a sports field, in a park. He is in a jacket at his desk, at a garden centre, at a cafe. "It has taken us 12 years to get the budget back on track. As much as we are passionate about a strong economy, it's actually why we're passionate about it that matters."

Morrison is a man without promise or promises. It is not clear why he wants to lead the country. He has yet to lay out a plan for it and gives no sign that he will. When he talks about Bill Shorten, he warns Labor will change everything. His own undertaking is that he will not. His proposition is the status quo.

Perhaps it is stability that drives a man such as this. More likely, it is ego. His ambition is not in question. His ambition for the country is. Each day of the election, it seems less likely that he has one.

"You change the government, you change the course of the country," he says. "And it takes a long time to get it back on track. So, that's what we're about."

It's a carnival trick, to sell you what you already have. Scott Morrison is staking the election on it.

Maybe God didn't make your penis

The defining feature of homophobia is that the people who hate you are picturing you having sex. Michael Kirby once made this point, although not as bluntly. The hatred is a kind of jealousy. The challenge of queer sex is a challenge to the notion that intimacy shared between a man and a woman is somehow special. It isn't.

This jealousy is the source of all the false reverence that exists for procreation. It is why critics of marriage equality talk about erosion: it's not a fear of difference so much as a fear that others can be like you. It's why conservatives hate being told that gender is a spectrum and it is not fixed. If being a man with a penis and a wife doesn't make you special, maybe you are not special. Maybe all the certainties of privilege and simplicity are constructs, too. Maybe God didn't make your penis. Maybe God didn't even make you a man.

This debate is not about Israel Folau. This debate is about the viciousness with which a segment of society will define itself as morally superior to another. In the past week, ordinary Australians have spent a few million dollars to confirm this prejudice.

Likely, a religious freedom bill will follow. David Marr writes that the argument around it is arrogant and contradictory. "Here's a simple principle: being decent and kind requires no legislation," he writes. "You only need a religious freedom act to shelter behind when you plan to be nasty." And: "If you are demanding rights for yourself which you won't extend to others, that's not freedom. It's privilege."

The freedoms being sought are not to practise but to persecute. They are about punishing people whose difference is necessary to sustain the righteousness of believers. This should be controversial but it's not, really. Too much of the world shares or accepts the hate that underpins it.

That's what this is: it is a reminder that enough of Australia harbours contempt for queer people that a special law to allow for their mistreatment can be recommended to the parliament and that can be thought of as normal. It is a reminder that the lives of queer people are expendable in debate. Our politics has made a recent art of it.

Before the election, Scott Morrison spoke of family as the building block of society. He quoted Robert Menzies. He was talking about shifting the country back to a time before identity became complex, before inclusion became a principle that challenged the primacy of people like him.

People who fear queerness fear being told they are not superior. They fear a world without the certainties that make them comfortable and put them in charge. This is about the power of chauvinism and the fragility of privilege. It is about the limits of imagination.

The people fundraising for Folau would pay for the right to call homosexuality a sin and say that it is taking over the world. They are paying for the right to say that the devil makes a child trans. They are paying for the right to condemn others to hell.

The ideas in all this are easy enough to abstract, but only if you don't care about people.

Destroying Australia

And so it passes, the greatest assault on the safety net from which Australian life is built. Scott Morrison's tax cuts are through and the revenue base that provides for health and education and social welfare is shredded. The legacy of the 46th parliament is there in its very first week: the destruction of the social compact that made this country stable.

On analysis by the Grattan Institute, to pay for these cuts at least $40 billion a year will need to be trimmed from government spending by 2030. The Coalition argues it will not cut services. It says jobs growth will reduce spending on welfare. A surplus will mean less interest paid on debt.

The assumptions are heroic and unsustainable. They show an extraordinary indifference to reality. More than that, they are indifferent to need. People will be worse off under these cuts. They will face greater hardship, have less access to health and to quality education. The people worst affected did not vote for Scott Morrison. Half the country didn't. The damage done is near irreversible. It is infinitely easier to cut taxes than to raise them. This is a triumph of greed and political cowardice. The Labor Party waved it through.

The principles of this policy were first written on a paper napkin in 1974, when the conservative economist Arthur Laffer sketched out his famous tax curve for Dick Cheney and Donald Rumsfeld. That serviette is one of the most pernicious documents in modern politics. It made the case for what became trickle-down economics. It became the lie through which governments gave money to the rich and pretended they were helping the poor.

The year Scott Morrison became treasurer, the Australian Chamber of Commerce and Industry brought Laffer to Australia for a speaking tour. He met with Josh Frydenberg. His doctrine has its most explicit contemporary expression in the cuts passed this week.

We know this doesn't work. In 2012, the United States Congressional Research Service found no correlation between tax cuts for the rich and economic growth. It had 65 years of real data on which to draw. All but the most optimistic readers of the Laffer napkin agree on what is self-evident: giving money back to the rich serves only to increase inequality. It makes the rich richer.

In his first major speech as prime minister, Morrison said he didn't believe people should be taxed more to improve the lives of others. He said people had to work for it: they had to have a go. "I think that's what fairness means in this country," he said. "It's not about everybody getting the same thing. If you put in, you get to take out, and you get to keep more of what you earn."

This is a fundamental misunderstanding of the purpose of taxation. You don't pay tax in exchange for services. You pay tax for a society. Under Morrison, you pay less tax and you have less society. The obliterating self-interest of this week will be felt for generations. Morrison's victory is a huge, huge loss.

On Tim Fischer

Tim Fischer used to send a note to new members of parliament. It was a letter of advice, broken into nine points, for the career to which they had just been elected.

"On entering parliament," the first point read, "write down 10 names of close non-political friends you want to have still at the end of your career and if you have not had contact with them by Cup Day each year, you initiate contact to keep the friendship alive."

Some of the points went to decency. Others covered political advantage. He encouraged MPs to choose one country in Asia and engage with it deeply, especially in opposition. He said they should read local papers and develop knowledge in a specific policy area. "As part of this," he wrote, "keep a filing cabinet drawer for a chronology file and related reports in respect of each big issue, eg. a key rail corridor or a dam project or black spot mobile phone areas."

The advice finished, "Enjoy it all."

Fischer died this week, aged 73. The former Nationals leader was sick with an acute form of leukaemia. Many remembered him as idiosyncratic. It was a way of acknowledging that his graciousness and civility is uncommon in politics. Perhaps, even, it was out of place. Fischer stood out because he was so tall but also because he was so scrupulous. He understood service and made a life from it.

When John Howard announced his gun buyback, it was Fischer who joined him and stared down his own constituency. He did so not because Howard needed the numbers but because it was right. He argued with Nationals voters in towns where his own effigy hung.

Fischer was wrong about gay rights and native title, but he was right about Pauline Hanson. He stood up to One Nation where Howard bowed to opportunity. On race, he said the party was "divisive, dumb and wrong".

He was an internationalist trade minister, at odds with protectionists in his ranks. He spoke against the war in Iraq and argued for action on climate change. Later, he was an advocate for the Svalbard Global Seed Vault in Norway. "What drives me," he said, "in many ways – the clock is at four minutes to midnight with regard to biodiversity of plants."

Fischer retired from politics to be with his young sons. While many say that, he meant it. "Because I married later in life, happily, to Judy," he said, "I have an absolute, intense feeling about doing all I can to contribute to that marriage and to Dominic and Harrison's development."

Fischer's eldest son has autism, which contributed to the decision. Later, Fischer said he believed he had a mild form of autism himself.

When people say Fischer was eccentric, some of them mean he liked trains. Others are finding a way to note that he seemed unembarrassed by his tenderness. To look now at the National Party and think he once led it is to be reminded of how badly our politics has declined.

The untold joke

At best, larrikinism is a cover for the worst aspects of the Australian character. It excuses poor behaviour and indulges second-rate talent. It is a particular kind of unseriousness that avoids difficult questions and laughs at those who try to ask them.

Larrikins entrench the status quo by pretending to mock it. They keep in place this country's fear of difference. It is no accident that all larrikins are men and all of them white. It is only through privilege that a person gets by on lazy jokes and terrycloth.

Ita Buttrose says she misses it. She misses Paul Hogan. She misses "spontaneity" in the workplace. She says the conversations she used to have with Frank Packer wouldn't happen anymore. "We're far too sensitive, I think."

The chair of the most important cultural institution in Australia, the ABC, thinks political correctness has gone too far. "There are very few larrikins anymore ... We've sort of suppressed that side of our character," she says. "And I think we need to bring back the larrikin element of Australia and be very proud of it because it's very unique to us."

In an editorial, *The Australian* complains that "the public space for humour is now woke and bespoke". Clive James is old and Bill Leak is dead. According to the newspaper, rebelliousness and irreverence are being killed. "At a time of rampant identity politics, young warriors forget the gains. Bit by bit, laws are altered, petty grievances are legitimised, normalised."

Twice in the same leader, the newspaper complains about diversity. It says it is a progressive religion. There is a notion that to flirt with bigotry is brave – that, as *The Australian* puts it, "crossing the threshold of offence is the job description for these wild souls".

But they are not crossing any threshold, they are not tearing down hegemony, they are trying and failing to keep the fences in place. The radicals and larrikins are mocking those who step out of line, who want the world to be different.

What is it that these people want to say but can't? How much more awful could it be than what they already print?

It is hard to imagine the cartoons Bill Leak didn't publish. It is difficult to see what restrains *The Australian* in its campaign against trans children. For those who miss "spontaneity" between sexes, picture maybe the people who now feel safe to go to work.

When we complain about political correctness, we are complaining about equality. We are not mourning the untold joke: we are sore at the fact the room has changed, and there are people in it to take offence.

To pretend that Australia is built on larrikinism is to be satisfied with a culture of subservience, a culture built on cringe and false confidence. The larrikins are the ones who tell us to laugh something off, because that's better than changing it. The larrikins are cowards who keep the past in charge.

This is an emergency

We don't know for sure if Nero played violin while Rome burnt. If it did happen, it was likely a different instrument, perhaps a kithara. But that other question – of whether a leader could be so frivolous and uncaring in the face of such catastrophe – was answered this week by Scott Morrison.

Eventually, rosin on his hands, the prime minister said the smoke in Sydney was "deeply troubling" for "families and kids". He blamed the drought and the dryness of the bush. He said Australia's climate policies couldn't affect the weather. "I acknowledged earlier this year, in February, that climate change, along with many other factors, contribute to what is occurring today."

Anthony Albanese is no better. He is spruiking the market for coal. He is worried about Labor's future, not the country's. We have a government incapable of leadership and an opposition unable to oppose.

The world faces a great disaster. It is drying out and burning. There are floods and extinctions. The reefs are bleaching. Sea levels are rising. Refugees move across borders in greater and greater numbers. It is clear now that we will see in our lifetimes wars we might never have imagined.

The science says all this could still be arrested. The politics says it can't be. It is worse than cynicism. It is a mass failure of caring, a misalignment of values. We are trapped in a continuous, declining present. We have no sense of the future and no leaders who will take us there.

In Madrid, Angus Taylor argues for carryover credits, so that the government might do less. The world is slowly ending and he is doing a card trick. He is not even doing it well, and has to ask the other countries if they will pretend they didn't see him cheating.

Morrison's emptiness was made for another time. The world is too complicated for a man with no ideas. His only interest is comfort, which is why he cannot understand urgency.

When Robert Menzies was in office, having no policies was a virtue: there was nothing to weigh down the country as it rode the post-war boom. This is the model Morrison has borrowed. He looks to Menzies for guidance and 70 years later sees nothing to update.

It is hard to know a way through this. The government is patently ill-prepared for the calamity it faces. There is an emergency and it is being treated as a game. The electorate is too divided and nothing is being done to mend it. The sly maths of a majority is all the prime minister cares about – the opposition, too.

Something needs to happen, something drastic and soon. The sky is burning orange and something needs to happen. The air is on fire. This is wartime and the government we elected is our enemy. The whole country needs to face this together.

After the Great Fire, Nero built his palace in the ruins. Scott Morrison doesn't have that kind of imagination. He doesn't know what's next and his inability to conceive of it stops him from confronting what is happening now. This is the great, great failure of our time, and it will ruin the earth.

Respect and a little bit of fear

There is something in the Australian psyche that craves punishment. Perhaps it is in the fact that White Australia began as a penal colony. Perhaps there is a deeper thread of inferiority and submission in the British settlement.

Whatever it is, the society we have is an orderly one – deeply so. We created the myth of the larrikin so we might feel less bad about our deference to power. He is a sort of court jester who makes the draconian more comfortable.

Elections are routinely run on law and order because the giving up of rights is broadly popular. This is a reality Australians shy from, except when they're voting. For a country unused to good government we are enthusiastic about its overreach.

In New South Wales, police now have quotas to search people and move on others. They call these "proactive strategies". This financial year, they will conduct 237,089 searches. Some will be strip-searches. Some will be conducted against minors. Few will turn up results.

Police set these targets. They hoped for 241,632 searches last financial year, but fell short by a couple of thousand. There is no evidence the targets reduce crime. If anything, they distract police and malign the community.

On Thursday, Nicholas Cowdery, QC, told *The Sydney Morning Herald* that the quotas created a "great potential for abuse of power". The state's former director of public prosecutions said the "natural human response will be to seek to meet the target by proper or improper means – by fudging, by exercising power where it is not properly warranted".

Most potently, he said the targets were "a political exercise on the part of the police and, consequently, on the part of the government".

Policing is political. An ugly triangle links the tabloid media to the police force and the police to government. All benefit each other. Powers asked for are almost never denied. Results are of little consequence. Fear is useful and perception is everything.

Surveillance is a comfort in this world. The federal government campaigns on it. While much policing is state-based, the Coalition has put bureaucrats in uniform and turned departments into quasi-military outfits. They know this is popular. It is the premise of our immigration system and the mass incarceration of First Nations people.

Occasionally the law impedes our desire to be controlled. Twenty years ago, when the country began on its fetish for drug dogs, new acts had to be written. Covenants of civil and political rights stood in the way. The dogs are hugely ineffective, but they make us feel safe. The small quantities of mostly marijuana they take off the streets remind us of the government's pettiness and our own willingness for submission.

Ombudsmen have criticised this from various angles, and the answer has been more drug dogs. As with other searches, the targets are often marginalised. The comfort Australians feel around punishment is built on the knowledge it will be a particular class of people who are punished: the Indigenous, the poor, the mentally unwell.

An inquiry into strip-searches is yet to give its findings in NSW. It has heard traumatic accounts of children stripped naked without guardianship, of teenagers forced to bend over and expose their body cavities to waiting constables.

Police have been ignorant of the laws under which they work. Their operations have been defined by enthusiasm and incompetence. Confronted by this, the police commissioner defended his officers. He said people need to understand consequences. "They need to have respect and a little bit of fear for law enforcement."

What he is describing are the elements that make policing a political tool: respect and a little bit of fear. It has served our leaders for 200 years and made the country thoughtless, anxious and contented.

Panic! At the Costco

Really, we should not be surprised. Panic buying isn't an aberration – it's the logical extension of a political system based entirely on selfishness and indifference, on the hoarding of wealth and property. It is what happens when government persuades the public that it is the problem.

It is difficult to remain credulous as Scott Morrison says hoarding is one of the most disappointing responses to coronavirus. "Stop doing it," he says. "It's ridiculous. It's un-Australian … That is not who we are as a people."

Perhaps Morrison doesn't remember his election campaign launch last year. He's not alone. Few lines proved enduring, although this one is: "I will not punish Australians for taking responsibility for themselves and their families."

Morrison's society is one where people look after themselves first. The path is a clear one, he says. "Create a life and a family together. Work even harder to support them and give them the choices and hopefully an even better life than the one that you have."

He nods occasionally to supporting others, but for the people in this world it is always an afterthought. There is a simple refrain, which his parents followed: "They saved, they planned."

Morrison's promise has always been lower taxes. More money for you, and less for them. He says life is not about what you accumulate, then outlines the simple, honest and decent aspirations of people who want more than what others have.

And then, a year later, having triumphed on the promise of greed, he says: "Stop hoarding. I can't be more blunt about it. Stop it. It is not sensible, it is not helpful."

Crises are greeted by the best and worst in people, and the worst in people is what put this government in power. They won on grift and seem surprised the country doesn't trust them. You cannot reassure a public you've never succeeded in leading.

This isn't just Scott Morrison. The contraction of government services across decades has left people isolated and mistrusting. They have been told to depend on themselves, and that is what they are doing. A government that won't promise healthcare or education can't be expected to guarantee groceries.

The ungenerous spirit that empties shelves is acting on the absence of leadership we have been offered.

Morrison believes his success is in being an everyman. It is an everyman who goes to the football when the prime minister shouldn't. It is an everyman who addresses the nation and says "stop it" like he is scolding a child.

Everymen go on the holidays they've planned. They make promises to their children. Their choices are simple because they believe their lives are simple.

Everymen are ordinary, like Scott Morrison promises to be ordinary. The problem is ordinary people cannot lead countries. They don't have the capacity, don't have the insight or the empathy. They cannot reassure because they have nothing large enough – intellectually or emotionally – to draw on for reassurance. Scott Morrison is proof of that. Panic buying is proof of that. The many people who suffer from this virus will be proof of that.

We shouldn't judge the people lining up outside supermarkets or fighting in grocery store aisles for toilet paper, but we should judge harshly the celebration of greed and selfishness that put them there.

The sheer scale of it

Perhaps the government simply cannot visualise it. It is possible they are unable to fathom what is happening, to appreciate its size.

Certainly, that is the impression Stuart Robert gave when the myGov website crashed under the weight of 100,000 people trying at once to ask for help.

"My bad," the minister for Government Services said, "not realising the sheer scale of the decision on Sunday night by national leaders that literally saw hundreds and hundreds of thousands, maybe a million, people unemployed overnight."

Somehow, Robert makes his culpability sound like indignation. For a sentence that starts in the first person and finishes with a million desperate citizens, there is no doubt as to which end of the scale has his empathy.

Everywhere, the lines outside Centrelink were likened to the dole queues of the Great Depression. The image is neat but it is also right. "Life is changing in Australia, for every Australian," the prime minister, Scott Morrison, said. "And life is going to continue to change. For many, young and old, 2020 will be the toughest year of our lives."

In the face of this, Morrison is talking about haircuts and barre classes. At a time of great national crisis, he confesses he doesn't know what the latter is or how to say it. This might suggest it is an odd point of focus for a press conference about public health.

Morrison has special rules for personal trainers and wants shopping centre food courts to remain open for takeaway. He has decided twice as many people can go to a funeral as a wedding. He says all jobs are essential because it is essential to have jobs.

Morrison's response to this crisis is piecemeal and shambolic. His press conference on Tuesday night was the sort of policy improvisation that could have started with the words "Yes, and ..." Two weeks ago he was going to the football.

The prime minister is balancing the health of the public against the health of the economy, and doing neither very well. Each is hurting the other. What is needed in both areas is large-scale and decisive action.

We need radical measures to limit the spread of the virus. If a shutdown is necessary, the prime minister should stop nibbling at the edges of one.

If the government is willing to make comparisons to the Great Depression, it must envisage a comparable response. National building projects must be started and people employed in them. Money must be borrowed and we must consider that the tax cuts that have not yet come into effect should not come into effect.

The other lessons of the Great Depression must be learnt, too. Work must be done to pre-empt deprivation and the spike in suicides that came after 1929. The words Morrison speaks now are important and they must be about inclusion and social cohesion.

Perhaps on the other side of this we will be a society more aware of vulnerability. Perhaps we will care more for the old and the sick. Perhaps we will understand better the lives of the poor.

These things are by no means given. To start with, we need a prime minister who can speak with clarity and compassion, and guide us through.

A charter of hope

It is tempting to believe Australia will emerge from this crisis a kinder and fairer country, that something will come from the common experience of isolation, that our obvious frailty will make us gentler and more compassionate.

It is tempting but by no means given. From these odd, unnumbered days will emerge a country changed but not necessarily better. It will be the work of the next few weeks that decides if Australia is remade or shoddily put back together. The difference is immense.

If we are to be a hopeful country, we must find a way to express that hope. This is a job for writers, to say who we are and what we believe – to listen to the country's better nature and set it in prose.

This should be done on paper. We are a country without a bill of rights or a history of orators to define us. Our values are too often vague or imagined. Our politics is built on the likely and half-remembered.

The document need not be long, but it needs to be written and shared. It needs to say what is important to this country and implore our leaders to treat those values as a blueprint for the reality that follows the one we are now in.

Twenty-one years ago, John Howard attempted to draft a national preamble. Les Murray was called to assist but no poetry survived the process. An early version diminished Indigenous Australians and chided "fashion or ideology". The final copy began: "With hope in God, the Commonwealth of Australia is constituted as a democracy with a federal system of government to serve the common good."

Howard's preamble failed because it failed to imagine Australia as it was or as it would be. In the end the words were so cautious and reluctant that they read as if they were showing through from another page.

The document we need now must conceive of Australia as one whole with many parts. It must be founded on a broad understanding of dignity. It must remove the caveats used to describe inequality as fairness. It must recognise injustices and seek to heal them.

Scott Morrison has begun the vague work of patriotism. Confronting the coronavirus, he said: "This is a Team Australia moment." In his address to the nation, he said: "We'll get through this together, Australia ... I know we'll all do our bit."

These words are a start but they mean too little to be an answer. This may be deliberate. It cannot be left uncorrected.

In this time of common separation we need to find words of agreement. We need a language of shared purpose. It is unlikely our leaders will ask for it and so we must write it ourselves.

It won't be the work of one writer but many, bound together by urgency and optimism, inventing a future for the country, a charter of hope.

Radio silenced

If 2GB was a crime family – if you can imagine it – Ray Hadley would be a violent foot soldier and Alan Jones would be the plotting, vengeful don. Ben Fordham would be adopted as a favour to his parents.

With Jones's retirement, radio loses an ugly voice. It loses a little of its racism and some of its misogyny. It loses some antique slurs and curious bigotry and graphic rhetoric. Most of this will be replenished or reimagined. Like sunlight, prejudice is inexhaustible.

What won't easily be replaced, and what made Jones different, is his capacity to manipulate power. There is no one waiting to step into the misproportioned parlour of his influence.

Jones was twice failed as a politician. The Liberal Party was willing to have him, but voters would not. Yet few understand political power the way Jones did. Some broadcasters would berate a politician on air, but almost none would continue to do so in private. An even smaller number would get results from this.

Jones had the capacity to make it seem that the prime minister needed him more than he needed the prime minister. Most made this trick look easy for him. Some politicians hand-wrote their letters to Jones, because they knew he liked it better. If he wore a ring, they would kiss it.

When Jones announced his retirement, Scott Morrison phoned in. "You've always spoken your mind to everyone, including me," the prime minister said, "and we've had one or two disagreements, but you've always done the right thing for your country."

Jones worked from a place of false indignation. The world was unfair to him and to his listeners. "Oh, there's fucking dust in this studio," he yelled once, in a leaked tape. "If it was bloody John Laws or someone, the whole joint would be cleaned out. It's fucking ridiculous."

Jones's suffering was grandiose and so was his life. He was always hectoring and corralling. He would have his private butler write the name of his network in the top of his soup, in cream. It made him feel better. His socks matched his tie and his tie matched his pocket square. His outlook matched the curtains.

Jones hated progressives and loved the coarse idiom of his youth. He liked words that came from the farm. He liked backhanders and chaff bags. He was fulsome on the subject of shame. Women went without names and Muslim men were vermin. Sometimes he would apologise but never would he choose to.

Jones stood in the way of a carbon price and against tax reform. Research was not a feature of his show. It cost him in defamation payouts and deprived his audience of truth. He liked Optus and Qantas and received undisclosed incentives for saying so. He was instrumental in the Cronulla riots.

Jones is the end of something. Media will not again invest so much power in one person. Nor will politicians. Audiences are too fragmented. Networks are too weak. The influence he had was illusory, held over from a time when his ratings meant more and the residents of what he called Struggle Street could help win elections.

Advertisers recognised that they could do without Jones, which is part of why he is giving up. Politicians were slower to realise this, although they would have eventually.

If 2GB was a crime family, Jones would go now to tend his vegetables. Instead he will appear on Sky News and write columns for *The Daily Telegraph* and The Australian. But his power, mercifully, finally, is gone.

Eight minutes in America

It's my face, man.
I didn't do anything serious, man.
Please.
Please.
Please, I can't breathe.
Please, man.
Please, somebody.
Please, man.
I can't breathe.
I can't breathe.
I can't breathe.
Please.
[Inaudible.]
Man, can't breathe. My face.
Just get up.
I can't breathe.
Please, I need my [inaudible].
I can't breathe. Shit.
I will.
I can't move.
Mama.
Mama.
I can't.
My knee.
My nuts.
I'm through.
I'm through.
I'm claustrophobic.
My stomach hurt.
My neck hurts.
Everything hurts.
Some water or something.
Please.
Please.
I can't breathe, officer.
Don't kill me.
They gon kill me, man.
Come on, man.

I cannot breathe.
I cannot breathe.
They gon kill me.
They gon kill me.
I can't breathe.
I can't breathe.
Please, sir.
Please.
Please.
Please, I can't breathe.

No hope of help

In politics, some things are accidental. Some only start that way.

Perhaps when they began designing JobKeeper, the government couldn't remember what casual work entailed. Perhaps they simply forgot there were migrants here on temporary visas. It is only a million or so people between the two groups.

Certainly, they could not have intended for the program to cover priests. If the program was to prevent sackings, the government was indifferent to the church's record.

The drafting was vague, also, on whether the diocese could ask for half the wage back – to "assist with future payments and the balance sheet".

As a senior Catholic Church employee told the ABC: "For the church to use these funds in this way, while so many others in their community are excluded from JobKeeper or are seriously struggling financially at the moment, is simply shocking."

These things look like accidents, until they're not.

The decision to exclude universities from the scheme was deliberate. It is hard not to imagine the enmity at the root of this.

It's less than two years since the Morrison government cut $328.5 million from research funding for universities. According to some figures, the money for research and development is at its lowest in 40 years. Sometimes accidents are convenient.

Although a package is lately touted for the arts, the decision to starve the sector for three months was also deliberate. The government rejected calls for assistance. When JobKeeper came in at half its budget, they rejected them again.

This is the same government that tried to destroy the Australia Council, that cut funding to individuals and chipped away at national institutions with a series of specious efficiencies. The culture is stricken, and the government does not care.

Some arts companies could still fail, especially mid-sized ones – the ones where more radical work might be shown. Some artists will simply have stopped making art. The starving artist will have become starved.

These things might look like accidents, except that they are not. Why would a government that disdains experts want to fund their work when a shutdown could simply end it? Why would a politics that defies parody want to put money in the theatre?

Australia has been in a stubborn, decades-long culture war. This pandemic has been a Russian winter for the right. The true damage will not be known for years.

Instead they saved the Dish

The same week Sussan Ley refused to give protection to the Djab Wurrung trees, she gave special heritage status to the Parkes radio telescope. This is how culture is preserved in Australia.

Ley reasoned that the telescope was a symbol of science and inquiry. It had helped broadcast the moon landing, she said, and later inspired a film by Rob Sitch. "The most famous Dish in the nation," she called it, "... conserved and protected for future generations after being awarded National Heritage status."

It is as if the country is a Planet Hollywood and its heritage is a glass case with Roy Billing's jacket in it. Everything is simpler that way.

Four days earlier, Ley rejected an application to give heritage protection to an area of land near Mount Ararat, including six trees that are of particular significance to the Djab Wurrung people. The logic is difficult to fathom.

She left in place an order that is not binding and found that the tree most in the way of a road expansion is in fact not important. It will be torn down. By best estimates, this destruction will make the journey from Melbourne to Adelaide two minutes faster.

There is an alternative route for this road, although it was rejected. Ley wrote that even if the new route saved all trees, it "would come at a significant economic cost ... and would also delay the enjoyment of the road safety benefits".

The trees are known as *delgug* – "tall person". In their application to the Commonwealth, the Djab Wurrung Heritage Protection Embassy said the trees are living beings of immeasurable value. "These trees are our ancestors and we must protect them to the best of our ability. Destroying them is severely upsetting, and brings bad fortune."

When you visit the trees you cannot ignore their vastness, the awe of their swollen and hollowed trunks, the life and the living to which they have been witness. The decision to cut down one of them and run a kink of road perilously close to others is extraordinary.

To make sense of it, you have to look into the Australian psyche. This is the unfinished business of colonisation. It's so ingrained, ministers are likely unaware of it. But somewhere, deep

down, they would prefer to destroy what was here than to grapple
with the realities of taking it. Michael Kennedy, the lawyer for the
Djab Wurrung Heritage Protection Embassy, calls it
"institutional denial and institutional control".

As all this is happening, the Andrews government is in a
treaty process with First Nations people. Sissy Eileen Austin, a
Gunditjmara Keerraay Woorroong Djab Wurrung woman, is an
elected member in those negotiations. She says the latest decision
has "created a tidal wave of anxiety". She says: "Much of the last
887 days has consisted of Djab Wurrung warriors protecting
Country and fighting an endless battle in multiple forms." A
spokeswoman for the government says: "It's now time to get on
with this vital project, which will improve safety for communities
in Western Victoria."

A foot high in poster paint

It is possible that when Tony Abbott stood on the lawns of Parliament House in 2011, in front of a sea of cardboard signs and conspiracy theories, he changed the Liberal Party forever. At that No Carbon Tax Rally, he welcomed into the party a kind of madness.

This would be the end of expertise, the end of consensus and the end of public good. It would be the beginning of a new conservatism that was reactionary and nothing else.

Abbott stood in front of a brace of Coalition members and said: "As I look out on this crowd of fine Australians I want to say that I do not see scientific heretics. I do not see environmental vandals. I see people who want honest government."

In the crowd were members of the League of Rights and the National Civic Council. They were calling for an end to multiculturalism and the punishment of "illegals". Politicians were "fraudulent criminals". Taxes belonged up their "ass". These views weren't concealed from Abbott: they were written in poster paint, a foot high in front of him.

Later, the then opposition leader called the group "a representative snapshot of middle Australia". This is the lie at the heart of the contemporary Liberal Party: the pretence that the fringe has become the centre. One of the protest promoters, a Sydney broadcaster, had previously been sacked for showing his penis to colleagues. The rally had a similar feel.

"I want the protest to be civil," Abbott said in a subsequent press release, in which he regretted the abusive language of a few. "I want it to be entirely in keeping with the Australian tradition. But let's not get too precious about these things."

A straightish line can be drawn between that March day and Craig Kelly's campaigning for hydroxychloroquine, against all medical advice. Kelly, the member for Hughes, is part of the wing of the Liberal Party that believes expert consensus is a cause for doubt. He accuses medical officers of having "misled the Australian public" on the treatment of Covid-19.

As on climate change, ideology has rotted the brains of these people. The lens they have through which to interpret the world is curved by culture wars that can make no sense of health emergencies or environmental catastrophe.

Kelly has become a small celebrity in the internet's out-country. He has reached the conspiracy theorists of QAnon via the bleached teeth of Pete Evans. He has undermined the public health of the country, and no one in his party has spoken against him.

"There are many sides of this parliament who express individual views," the Health minister, Greg Hunt, says, missing the point or deliberately avoiding it. "We see that in relation to all parties at all times, that's one of the democratic freedoms, but our medical decisions are based on medical advice."

In London this week, Tony Abbott was musing again. He thought it was time for individuals to determine how they approach the virus. He complained that we have let fear keep us from being fully alive, forgetting that the alternative for some is being dead.

This shouldn't be mistaken for intellectual curiosity. With Abbott and Kelly, that's no great risk. This is a question of mischief and irrelevance – and it is one that puts in danger the community response required to combat the pandemic.

This man must be freed

We cannot print his name. We know he has been in immigration detention for seven years. We know his weight has dropped to 45 kilograms. He could die within weeks.

The government's medical contractors say his condition is critical. Their assessment is plain: "at risk of death from sudden cardiac death, organ failure, overwhelming infection or other effects of prolonged starvation".

The United Nations Human Rights Committee has carried out an "interim measure", urging the government to release him into the community. It has been ignored. The government does not care about his case.

In photographs the man looks like a Goya etching. His skin is loose and his skeleton is showing through. A bulldog clip holds up his trousers. He has a burning pain in his bones, which friends worry is the leaking of calcium into his blood.

For six weeks, his lawyers have been negotiating with the department. They offered to keep the story out of the press: this is not a protest, it's a medical issue. He is not on a hunger strike; he is simply too unwell to eat.

"No one with any decision-making power will meet with me directly," his lawyer says. "When it's a man's life – moving away from the medical and the law – it's just heartless and spineless."

Last year, he was placed in psychiatric care. After three months, it was recommended he not be returned to detention. The department refused. An attempt was made to deport him. His psychiatrist was not informed and nor was his lawyer. It only ended when he stood up on the plane and declared he was too sick to fly.

For seven years, he has been moved from centre to centre. This is done to detainees to ensure their networks do not become too established. Guards told him he would make new friends. He is scared that if he publicises his case, he will be punished. He believes this is what happened to the Biloela family. He does not want to go back to Christmas Island.

The man's refugee application has been rejected. The department claims his case was flagged by Interpol. Twice now, Interpol has said it has no record of him. The department has not responded. The phantom notice could cost this man his life.

The only option left is ministerial intervention. The question is no longer whether this will stop the boats, or if that was ever necessary, but rather how many people should die before we accept the system has failed and that it needs to be dismantled. It seems neither major party has an upper limit.

Since 2000, at least 58 people have died in immigration detention. They have died as the direct result of policy designed to punish them for a crime that does not exist. They have died because these policies are built from cruelty and indifference, and the ministers responsible believe any compassion would compromise the system.

Australia will let a man starve to death because killing him is in service of a national obsession with the security of our borders. The depravity of this is a stain on us all.

Clown duels

Early in his presidency, or perhaps just before it, a video circulated of Donald Trump grappling with an older man on the edge of a wrestling ring. Trump coathangered the man and, when they were both on the ground, pretended to punch him over and over in the face. Later, he dragged him into the ring and with clippers and then a razor shaved him bald, the foam falling from the man's scalp and onto the shoulders of his suit.

It was disturbing to watch, not for the simulated violence but for the joy Trump took in the make-believe. His face glowed with machismo, as if he were unaware that it was all pretend – "that the reality he was in, the one where this bloated, ill-fitting man was a great fighter, had been entirely constructed. This week's presidential debate had the same feel but with lower production values.

Trump's great power is that he is completely unencumbered by the space between what is real and what is not. Sometimes this looks like the absence of shame, but it is more than that. His presidency is a continuous act of invention. Lies are inexhaustible and so the power he draws on will never run out.

People described feeling nauseated as they watched the debate. This was the sick feeling that comes from a loss of balance – from seeing the horizon line of what is true and real being bent in front of you. The nausea was not just at Trump's scrabbling braggadocio but also at Joe Biden's meek and sniggering ripostes.

Here on stage were two men who would lead the free world, neither of them with any worthy claim to it. Here were two jelly wrestlers at closing time, but without the integrity of the sport.

Debate under Trump has acquired a special shapelessness. Nothing has any great meaning or particular import, and so there are no priorities by which to be guided. Biden tried to correct this, but when he did he had nothing to say.

It is a cliché to note that democracy is in crisis, but it is. Without truth, or some cursory understanding of it, democracy cannot properly function. Trump knows this and he has staked on it his re-election.

Serious thinkers are now speculating on what happens if Trump does not accept defeat – how he might exploit uncertainties in the United States constitution, or other loopholes, to deny his loss. This would plunge the country into chaos. It is not clear how it would be resolved.

The argument might be excessively optimistic, however. There is still a chance he will win outright. In the same way that you can't argue with a drunk, you can't debate Donald Trump. He can will half a country into his own unreality and the best Biden can do is to call him a clown.

For Trump and his America the Californian fires are about smoking and coronavirus is about Big Ten football. Insulin is as cheap as water. In a circus such as this, a clown can lead the country – and pointing out that he is one doesn't change a thing.

Taylor's super grass

Imagine a federal minister who has a stake in a company alongside other members of his family. Imagine that company is accused of illegally poisoning more than 28 hectares of critically endangered grassland. Imagine the minister talks to senior officials in the office of the future treasurer.

Perhaps there is an intercept of the conversation. Perhaps a federal integrity commission is investigating claims the minister lobbied to have environmental protections removed while the treasurer was still minister for the Environment.

Imagine this commission asks a senior bureaucrat what he meant when he wrote "Minister keen to see [whether] he can accommodate Angus Taylor's requests ... Want a how to for Minister in event he wished to amend or delete thresholds." What did it mean in these notes, the commission might ask, when you drew a little arrow and wrote "need to know in advance if going to get a brief which does not support"?

Maybe this minister says he "never asked Mr Frydenberg to change laws governing the clearing of native grasslands". Maybe the commission might ask him straight: What were these requests, then?

Perhaps this same commission takes an interest in the sale of water rights to the government by a company connected to the minister. Perhaps it is able to subpoena financial records. Maybe it asks questions about the $80 million valuation, about why this was offered without tender, about whether any water has actually been acquired under the deal.

Maybe this commission would look at changes made to a document, purporting to be from the City of Sydney's website. Maybe the prime minister would be called as a witness and asked about an intervention he made with the New South Wales police commissioner. When you say friends, the commission might ask, what do you mean? What did you ask him on the call?

Perhaps another inquiry looks into the awarding of grants in marginal electorates, and asks what processes were followed and if any laws were breached. Maybe there is an inquiry into the purchase of land at Leppington, south-west of Sydney, from Liberal donors, at possibly 10 times its value. Maybe another looks at the use of electorate office staff to do party work.

The Saturday Paper is not suggesting an integrity commission would find evidence of misconduct in any of these cases. For that, it would have to exist.

The federal government has proposed a national integrity commission, but it is narrow and impotent and unlikely to be effective in exposing corruption. Its definitions are restrictive and its thresholds for investigation too high. An inquiry such as the one under way in NSW, the one that might yet cost a premier her job, would be doubtful under its terms.

Still, it's nice to imagine a federal government unafraid of standards. It's nice to imagine grant programs conducted with integrity and open to scrutiny, or ministers answerable for their actions, or a public served by politicians whose conduct was open to review and whose decency was assured by robust processes.

As it stands, the company Taylor part owns is appealing the findings against it. After three-and-a-half years, the environment department ordered Jam Land to remediate more than 100 hectares of damaged grassland. Taylor says it is a matter for the company and he does not have a controlling interest.

Genie in the subtle energy lamp

It's not only Pete Evans. He's just the untreated symptom of a politics that cannot deal with complexity. It is a politics without any real constituency, stretching and searching to find something that might give it power.

Evans exists in a place that mistakes conspiracy theories for independent thought. He backs multilevel marketing schemes and says fluoride causes "brain … diseases". In April he was fined by the Therapeutic Goods Administration for selling a lamp he said could treat "the Wuhan coronavirus". Every morning he stares directly into the sun.

This week, Evans was dropped by his publisher and television network after posting a neo-Nazi cartoon on Facebook. Stores sent back his books and products. In the image, a caterpillar in a Trump hat is drinking with a butterfly whose wings are marked with the sonnenrad. "You've changed," the caterpillar says. "We're supposed to," the butterfly says. "An oldie but a goldie," Pete Evans says.

The former television chef denies knowing what the drawing meant. Ignorance is not new for him. "The fact," he says, "that I had to actually Google what neo-Nazi meant is pretty telling." Earlier, he posted: "You may wish to have another look about the true history about Germany."

Evans doubts reality. He points his followers to mad theories. "Masks in the bin," he wrote this month. "Hugging for everyone. Vaccine to be replaced with organic food, plant medicines, sunlight … breathwork …"

Over time, far-right politics has intermingled with these crank remedies. In part, this is because they represent an anti-government movement. They promise a return to simpler times. Just as Nazism hid out in the occult after World War II, some sovereign citizens hide out in wellness.

It is a strange and inconsistent place, this fringe. They fear 5G and believe a one-world government is assembling in the shadows. They see paedophile networks everywhere, in pizza shops and empty railway tunnels.

That this fringe exists and is growing says a lot about the impoverishment of thought on the right. Jumbled up in the bone broth and black suns is a search for meaning and a rejection of change. Conspiracy theories are necessary for this thinking to cohere. Experts are derided. Righteousness is everywhere.

Figures from this fringe are present in office. A QAnon supporter won a United States house seat in the recent elections. In Australia, Liberal MPs support hydroxychloroquine treatments and post about "Democrat vote fraud".

But this fringe must be confronted. The disinformation needs to be countered. Adherents need to be deradicalised. It could start with the prime minister confronting conspiracy theories on the government's benches, although that seems unlikely.

For Evans, it's uncertain what happens next. Fans online are thanking him for speaking "truth". After losing his endorsements, he shared an image of a human eye in a galaxy of stars. "Awe, wonder, gratitude and curiosity," he wrote. "Always love and trust."

As with the cartoon, it's not clear that any of those words mean what he thinks they mean.

Without my pants

Scott Morrison's response to climate change is to take off his pants. It is not yet summer and his office has released pictures of him dressed for press conferences from the waist up. Below his jacket are a pair of shorts and rubber thongs. His legs are raw with mosquito bites.

This is intended to be endearing: the larrikin who'll wear a suit only if he has to, getting one over you on a Zoom call. Probably it works. In truth, it's a picture of a man who is never more than half prepared. What Scott Morrison thinks is clever is usually the opposite.

Morrison refuses to set a target for emissions reduction, although the reality is every state and territory already has. He says "the second half of this century", as if a 50-year window for net zero represents a shrewd piece of drafting and not the destruction of the planet.

At the G20 this week, he said "what we've set, we've met". As with his social policies, he mistakes rhyme for action. He's still talking the lie of carbon capture and the false transition of gas. The numbers he does have run out in a decade. Labor is little better.

Australia has a moment of opportunity: to join the rest of the world in addressing global warming, or to keep going with whatever school rugby trip Scott Morrison is on. External factors will force this decision and so the question is: Why doesn't Morrison just agree to what is obvious, if only to save what little face he has? Why doesn't he announce a target of net zero by 2050, and do what needs to be done? Surely the gains in Queensland – if that's what it is – are not worth the isolation in the world. Surely they are not worth the death and catastrophe that accompanies inaction.

John Kerry's appointment as America's special envoy for climate will put more pressure on Australia. Kerry will return the United States to the Paris agreement and re-engage Europe on higher commitments. Soon climate action will feature in trade agreements. Kerry will set it in national security terms, as he did as secretary of state. A moment of real change is near.

Kerry has already indicated that his approach to climate change will be international. "To end this crisis," he says, "the whole world must come together." He points to the Glasgow climate conference as a key moment next year: "All nations must raise ambition together or we will all fail together, and failure is not an option."

And then there is Scott Morrison, a fundamentally unserious person, standing in The Lodge without his pants and asking his mates if anyone on the call noticed.

On Mungo MacCallum

What made Mungo MacCallum special, one of the things, was that for all the bewilderment and dismay he felt looking at politics he never lost his sense of clarity. If John Howard was the most effective politician of the past two decades, Mungo's preferred description of him was the most enduring: "an unflushable turd".

MacCallum called his memoir *The Man Who Laughs* and he was, even with a politics built of bad news. The shape of his nose meant that when he was serious it still looked as if he was thinking of something funny. "I come from a political family," he wrote. "This is less of a boast than an admission." The descendant of explorers and conservative politicians, he had another gag about this: "I used to volunteer that two great Australian families met in me, and both lost."

MacCallum was part of a generation of writers who went to Canberra and changed the country. Robert Menzies was still in power. MacCallum's journalism made our politics vivid and stumbling and alive. As his publisher, Chris Feik, said this week: "He brought wit to the coverage of Australian politics, and thus permanently expanded our sense of it."

MacCallum was *The Saturday Paper*'s first employee. A year and a bit before our launch, he sent a message out of the blue: "Know anyone who wants a regular supply of cryptic crosswords?" MacCallum did not know that we were planning a newspaper, just that he had "a huge emotional and financial need for a new outlet". He took the job in three words: "Thanks mate – onboard."

In recent years, MacCallum survived a heart attack and emphysema, and fought three types of cancer. "Recuperating from pneumonia, emphysema, melanoma and Tony Abbott," he wrote in one message. "I'll give you a ring when things have settled down a fraction."

Surgery on his throat made it impossible to talk easily, although he never stopped writing. If an editor rang to check the meaning of a line, worried it might be defamatory, he would respond that this was indeed its intention: "A problem for you, my boy."

MacCallum wrote with speed and flair. There was never a column he couldn't deliver. Length and deadline were the only needed prompts. The final words would almost always be early: "Herewith."

Two weeks ago, MacCallum sent a note to his editors. "I never thought I'd say it, but I can no longer go on working," he wrote. "It takes all my effort to breathe and I'm not managing that too well. And now my mind is getting wobbly – hard to think, let alone concentrate.

"So I am afraid there is not much point in continuing to push the rock up the hill. I shall retire to my Lazy Boy recliner, and doze over the television watching (or not) old sporting replays, propped up by drugs, oxygen and the occasional iced coffee. I am rapidly winding down.

"I am sorry to cut and run – it has sometimes been a hairy career, but I hope a productive one and always fun. My gratitude for all your participation."

Mungo is survived by his partner, Jenny, his daughters Diana and Gail, his stepdaughters Adrienne and Gillian, and, by his estimate, "several million words' journalism". Last week he sent enough cryptic crosswords to last until March.

A useful excuse

The iconic image is of Kenneth Hayne in an office with Josh Frydenberg. The former High Court justice is presenting the treasurer with the final report of his royal commission into banking.

Hayne has the long, tired face of a basset hound who has been betrayed. His nose is the same colour as his tie. A photographer asks if the two men might shake hands. Hayne does not break eye contact with the table. He says, simply: "Nope."

Two years on, this grim photo opportunity is perhaps the most lasting outcome of the banking royal commission. An analysis by *Guardian Australia* shows that more than half of Hayne's recommendations are yet to be implemented. Some have been abandoned entirely. A photographer tried again, asking if Hayne could push the report across the desk towards Frydenberg. Hayne shook his head and began to stand up from his seat. "It's alright," the treasurer said. "It's just … It's done."

The old joke goes that inquiries are for having, not doing. It's not the strongest punchline but this is not the strongest government. For Scott Morrison, difficult issues are the preserve of royal commissions. They happen in a future he has not yet imagined. For as long as the inquiries run, they are a useful excuse for inaction.

Morrison has held royal commissions into aged care and natural disasters, the latter of which he chose instead of climate change. He has another running into the abuse and neglect of people living with disabilities. Some findings are already tabled and some will be delivered in the coming months.

What is being amassed is a catalogue of responsibilities. The prime minister's unimaginable future will arrive this year, no longer obscured by the pandemic or shaded by the influence of the banks. The government owes it to those who gave evidence to act on the recommendations.

For a government that won the last election without a platform, and which has been loath to develop policy since, these royal commissions provide a limited but necessary agenda. Of course, that requires a government willing to lead. It requires a prime minister who established the inquiries with the intent of acting rather than avoiding.

It is possible this will be an election year. If it is, and if between now and then the government does not find its purpose, it will be the fourth time the Coalition has gone to the polls without an agenda. Until now, the electorate has accepted this. Surely at some point, like Kenneth Hayne, unsmiling and rigid and misled, it will ask for more.

War games

Scott Morrison struggles to differentiate between the national interest and his own. This is not because the two are closely linked.

Morrison, perhaps more than any previous prime minister, is obsessed with elections. They are his perfect forum. He was a state party director before he was a politician and his footing always is for a campaign.

All prime ministers are focused to some degree on being returned to office, but for Morrison it is everything. The time between polling days is a nowhere space to him. There are no great, animating policy issues; there is just winning.

It is through this blinkeredness that we might understand Morrison's approach to China. It is not just naivety or brashness. It is a fundamental disjunct of scales: Morrison's seats and margins, calculated as if for a board game, against the seismic force of global tensions.

As with everything for Morrison, it is a failure of imagination. He cannot picture what might happen and so cannot see the terrifying folly of what is happening. He doesn't understand the risk in his escalations.

As Hugh White writes in today's edition: "The danger of war is very real, so this is no longer a hypothetical question ... The consequences for Australia, the region and the world would be devastating and it would fail to achieve the objective of preserving US leadership in Asia. On the contrary, it would destroy America's position in Asia."

The Morrison government will not force China to abandon its ambitions. It is not clear what tools it thinks it may have to do this. We cannot rely on the United States. Yet we have no real might of our own.

When Peter Dutton says Australia is "already under attack" the rhetoric is the same he used to militarise the immigration system. It worked against a small and imagined enemy. The difference, however, which the Defence minister cannot appreciate, is that this time it would be a real war, fought with guns and missiles, not with the lives of refugees.

When Mike Pezzullo talks about the curse of war, he does so still in the realm of dress-ups. In charge of uniformed customs officials, the secretary of Home Affairs reaches for grandeur. He intones on the "only prudent, if sorrowful, course – to send off, yet again, our warriors to fight the nation's wars".

Borrowing from history, he forgives Europe its sorrow but mourns its failure to "heed the drums of war which beat through the 1930s". He says: "War might well be folly, but the greater folly is to wish away the curse by refusing to give it thought and attention, as if in so doing, war might leave us be, forgetting us perhaps."

The link between these three men is more than politics; it is the panto fashion in which they practise it. When Morrison and Dutton talk of war footings, they think of the battle to win seats. Real war is not like that.

Political campaigns are rarely grand, strategic triumphs. More often, they are petty and small, won on tricks and schemes. Numbers are eked out at the margins, corflutes defaced or pamphlets snatched from letterboxes.

The reality Morrison now flirts with is quite different: large, uncertain and possibly nuclear. One dearly hopes he realises what is at stake.

Mass vax implosion

The Morrison government won't say how much Covid-19 vaccine there is in the country. They won't say to which states it has been sent or how much has been administered. When asked in private briefings, the answer is: "That's information in confidence."

There is no public data to say why the rollout has stalled, or if it was hubs that produced a record day for vaccinations this week, or to show if that was related to supply. There is no data to say what is working and what is not.

Epidemiologists are relying on unofficial sources to piece together information. What is freely available in New Zealand is not available here. Secrecy threads through the entire response.

"That's a sad testament to what information the government could be but is not giving," says Mary-Louise McLaws, an adviser to the World Health Organization on infection control for Covid-19.

"This builds up mistrust, and you don't want mistrust in an outbreak. My question is: Why would you sign an agreement that won't let the government tell the taxpayer what's going on? To me, it's a bad agreement Australia is signing if they can't tell taxpayers what has turned up." At another briefing, McLaws asked how many people by age group and phase had been vaccinated. That information is key to understanding uptake. "The answer was: It's too difficult."

Similarly, there is no federal data to show how many people in hotel quarantine have tested positive or on what day of their quarantine this has happened. The government directs researchers to the states, despite having legal responsibility.

"We need transparency of data: how much we were promised and how much has arrived," McLaws says. "Transparency makes for co-operation and trust. You don't get to fight a pandemic without trust and co-operation."

McLaws says there's an argument that the rollout should prioritise 20- to 39-year-olds, at least from an epidemiological standpoint. "They're young, mobile, sociable and they're looking for work," she says. "They're responsible for 50 per cent of cases in Australia. That's the group I would be targeting first. And then you get ads and campaigns that target those groups."

It is not clear what plan the government has for the rollout. The country is behind targets and has no way to meet them this year. Public health messaging is limited. Money has been spent with McKinsey and other private enterprises, but it is not clear what experts have been consulted. Hubs have been belatedly established, but their services are hugely undersubscribed. There is no information on how much vaccine has spoiled because of this. Once reconstituted, the Pfizer vaccine lasts only six hours.

It is hard to believe that the secrecy is just one of contracts. It is the secrecy of government incompetence, of saying nothing because there is nothing good to say. Where scrutiny is needed there is equivocation.

It is urgent for the government to make clear the process of the vaccine rollout, to accept its flaws and rebuild public trust. Information about supply should be published, as should vaccination rates by age group and location. There is a real prospect that without this, and a multipronged plan for mass vaccination, Australia will not reach herd immunity.

For the Morrison government, this is a political issue. For everyone else, it is about how we live. Both are forms of survival, but one should matter much more than the other.

Guilty of bravery

It is an absurd situation. Witness K has pleaded guilty for his role in exposing wrongdoing by the government. He is being sentenced over a crime Australia committed.

In a little room in Canberra, behind black panels to conceal his identity, he spoke his first words in open court: "Guilty, your honour."

A former spy, he was charged with conspiring to reveal information about an operation in which Australia bugged political offices in Timor-Leste to help rig negotiations over the country's oil and gas fields.

It was a craven exercise, wholly motivated by profit. Australia succeeded in exploiting an impoverished neighbour and delivered an enormous windfall for a private company. This was standover capitalism.

"Corporate greed was a big part of it," Timor-Leste's chief negotiator told *The Guardian* in 2019, "because the Howard and Downer government, they were shills for the corporations. That was what was really important to them."

The case against Witness K and his lawyer, Bernard Collaery, has dragged on for years. Almost all of it is secret. The government has prevented K from publishing a book, threatening him with jail. They have taken his passport to prevent him testifying at The Hague.

According to his barrister, he suffers "alienation, anxiety and post-traumatic stress". For his decency he has been gravely punished.

José Ramos-Horta, the former president of Timor-Leste, says this is "a story of chicanery, of innocence and trust betrayed". He calls Witness K and Collaery "brave Australians, individuals with a conscience and courage, representing the very best of Australians as I know them – instinctively sympathetic to the underdog, the weak and vulnerable". He says: "These men haven't done any harm to their country. They honoured Australia."

All of this is true. Australia acted unconscionably in Timor. The redrawn maritime boundary between the two countries is proof of this. The pursuit of the two men who exposed our malfeasance is a further crime.

Outside the Canberra courts, a group of protesters sometimes gathers in support of Collaery and Witness K. Sometimes they tape shut their mouths. One of their signs reads: "Charge the real criminals."

The sign doesn't say who these criminals are. It doesn't need to. For anyone who has followed this appalling saga, the answer is obvious.

To the Entsch degree

Fifteen years ago, Warren Entsch pushed three black-and-white photographs of a woman in lingerie across his desk. "There's my missus. Look at that," he told the journalist sitting opposite. "Good-looking bird and I love her to bits."

Entsch was pushing for same-sex marriage rights at the time. John Howard was still prime minister. The former crocodile hunter and bull catcher was being described as a pink redneck. The pictures were to prove he was taking up the cause for other people: he wasn't gay and he had two failed marriages and a new partner to prove it.

Entsch took an admirable stand, albeit through a confused, sometimes offensive line of reasoning. "They're usually young, pretty good-looking fellas," he said of the gay men he was representing, "and it gives us old fellas a chance at these good-looking young sheilas."

Entsch's new cause is the Great Barrier Reef. Two years ago, Scott Morrison made him the reef's "special envoy". It's a curious title in that it has no real meaning. Entsch says he is interested in how to "leverage many opportunities for economic growth". He won't be "hand-wringing about impending mass human extinctions". He says things like: "In my view helping the environment doesn't have to cost the earth!"

Entsch's new lingerie shots are misrepresented reports and faulty science. He slides them into radio interviews and across the desk to international officials. He claims the bleaching of the reef is worse because so much has been done to clean up the water – and sunlight gets through more easily. He says Australia is a "victim of our own success".

As part of a campaign to prevent the reef being listed as "in danger", he led a snorkelling trip to Agincourt Reef. The Environment minister, Sussan Ley, flew to Europe to lobby ambassadors. Both were arguing against their own scientists. The campaign was to save face and nothing else.

The pair succeeded, although the word is too generous. The United Nations will hold off in changing the reef's listing. They will consider the decision again next year.

This is not a win. Certainly, not for the reef. The level of bleaching is catastrophic. Rising temperatures will increase bleaching events until the reef is pushed past its capacity to regenerate. Without a concerted plan to address climate change, the whole, extraordinary ecosystem will eventually die. The fact that Entsch's answer to this is boat trips and pseudoscience is terrifying.

When Entsch worked at a crocodile park, his dog would get into the pens at night. Entsch would run out naked, waving a rake, trying to protect the dog from the crocodiles. "I often thought, if I slipped arse-over-head, what would the papers say in the morning about this kinky bugger naked in a crocodile pond with a dog?"

Entsch's stewardship of the barrier reef is similar: his response is flailing and insufficient; it makes no attempt to address the root causes; and mostly it is concerned about what the papers will say.

Moral stature

John Howard's wife once complained to a cartoonist that he was drawing her husband too small. She insisted Howard was the same height as Bob Hawke. In the cartoons, he seemed much shorter: head and shoulders below him. The cartoonist paused and then explained that what he was depicting was moral stature.

Howard of course led Australia into Afghanistan. His smallness was also aggressive. It had the insecurity of someone quite willing to follow others. From the outset, George W. Bush seemed to understand this.

Howard's smallness was hereditary. Tony Abbott has it, as does Scott Morrison. It is a smallness not just of morals but of imagination – a kind of satisfaction that comes with knowing the limits of your mind, and that you could walk them before breakfast.

Morrison's response to the fall of Afghanistan exemplifies this smallness. He has no interest in the situation because it is larger than him. There are no votes in it. The television news doesn't care. Even the readers of this newspaper are less interested than they are in the vaccine rollout. The traffic numbers prove it.

Morrison's lack of imagination has left behind thousands of people. Their fate is reasonably certain. The Taliban is not new and their actions are unlikely to surprise. As one Hazara refugee recounts in the paper this week: "Once the international forces are out of Kabul airport, the dark time will again come to Afghanistan. People know that. The Taliban is not new to Afghan people. We keep forgetting that: they are not a new regime. They were there before. They have already killed thousands of people in front of their families. It is just a matter of time. Straight away they will kill people. They will not ask questions. There is no mercy. The fear people have is that once the international forces leave Kabul airport, the Taliban will start slaughtering. People sense it. They know."

This makes it even more troubling that there was no evacuation plan. As Karen Middleton reports, a pro forma document was taken off a shelf. There was no attempt to get people from their homes to the airport, even people who had worked with Australian forces and were especially vulnerable because of this.

There was no special planning. Defence worked so quickly they didn't even have time to give the operation a name.

The rush came because of indifference, because Morrison couldn't be bothered with a plan. He couldn't see the point of one. The lack of urgency will be fatal. We will hear little about it.

This is the smallness of our politics. It is the smallness of Howard and Abbott and Morrison and others. The problem now is that in a cartoon you wouldn't notice: they're all the same size.

Same shame but different

This week, Danish politician Inger Støjberg was sentenced to two months in prison for illegally ordering the separation of migrant couples. This is an extraordinary form of accountability. It is more remarkable, however, when you consider Støjberg's policies were substantially modelled on Australia's.

Støjberg was immigration minister when the Danish government announced it would conduct a fact-finding mission to Nauru and Manus Island. She was the minister who proposed sending refugees to a small island in the Baltic Sea, previously used to conduct research on sick animals.

She taunted on Facebook that these refugees "will be getting a new address". She wrote, "When you are unwanted in Danish society, you should not be a nuisance for regular Danes."

It was Støjberg who thought to take out advertising in foreign countries, just as Australia had done, telling refugees not to come to Denmark. "The advertisements must contain sobering information about the halving of benefits and other constraints we are going to adopt," she said at the time. "This kind of information spreads."

It was Støjberg's idea to take jewellery from refugees who entered the country, using its meagre value to pay for their processing. Guards in the end refused. Of course, as with our own system, it was never about money: it was about taking away another little piece of a person's humanity, about making them a non-person. It was about taking what memories might exist in a thin gold chain and saying, "Your past is ours now and so is your future and we refuse to give you either."

There are small differences between Denmark and Australia. As minister, Støjberg lied about children at a childcare centre, saying they were banned from eating pork because of the pressure from Muslims. Here, Scott Morrison lied about staff on Nauru, saying they were "allegedly coaching self-harm and using children in protests".

The elements are common, however. The fears are the same: children being mistreated by an unknown other, either Muslims or activists. The Australian government ultimately paid compensation over Morrison's claims, but he never apologised. Nor did Støjberg, although she admitted she should have checked her lie. "It was a story I was told at a private party," she said, "by people who I trust."

When Støjberg passed her 50th law restricting immigration, she celebrated with a cake decorated with fruits and chocolate piping. There was grim whipped cream and a marzipan flag. Morrison marked his time in Immigration with a novelty trophy of one of the fishing boats that brought to this country the innocent men and women whose suffering he turned into political gain. Different slightly, but also the same: smug, cruel and morally gauche.

The fact of Støjberg's conviction is astounding. Essentially she is being punished for the viciousness of her politics. She will likely serve her sentence in the community, as is right. Morrison got three years, and spent it in The Lodge.

Because I said

Scott Morrison's smile is like a measuring tape. It lengthens as he decides what it is he can get away with. The calibration is sometimes off but this does not affect his confidence. Before he speaks, he sucks air hard through his nose: one last assessment, as if to smell the credulity of the room.

"Um, well," he said this week, "I'd have to check with Jen, because she, um, she's the one that goes and, and gets them, um, for, for those situations."

The question was simple enough: How many rapid tests have you personally paid for? What was really being asked was: Do you understand how difficult it is to get them, that symptomatic people are going from pharmacy to pharmacy because of a failure of supply?

The smile arrived as Morrison said his wife's name. The measuring began. Jen holds a special purpose in the Morrison government: she is a reminder that the prime minister is a husband first, that he governs from this position and that the sanctity of family means he will not give clear responses. Like all fathers, his final answer is *because I said*.

"When they're being used for private use, then Jen's popped around to the chemist or wherever she's gone," Morrison continued. "I think recently she went to one here in Canberra, um, for that reason, and was able to eventually find one. Just like everyone else, driving around looking to find one."

A few weeks ago, he claimed he bought his own test at a pharmacy in Terrigal. "Picked one up. Took the test. It was negative. I didn't need the government to tell me to do anything." Of course, that's not true: Morrison is the government. He waited in a Comcar while a staffer bought the test for him. He called this "a real-life example".

Morrison governs through anecdote. He lives entirely in the first person. He's in it, just like you. Except he's not. He's the prime minister. He shouldn't be driving around looking for tests. No reasonable person expects that. What he should be doing is making them available. If his wife is driving around looking for them it is not because he's on your side – it's because he's not. He has failed you and he has failed the country. If he wants to add Jen to the list of people he has let down in this pandemic, that's for him.

Morrison is fundamentally confused about the role of the prime minister. He remains a state party director at heart: he works for the people who voted for him, and no one else. This has been the fundamental failure of the pandemic. He never believed himself responsible for the country as a whole. Now he has failed even those who put him in charge.

Morrison's response is the same as it has always been: to smile and hope the country will look after itself; that he will continue life as the ordinary man who found himself miraculously prime minister, the King Ralph of Australian politics.

The halfway man

There is an argument that says prime ministers, whatever their qualities, tell the story of the country that elected them. Australia was brash like Bob Hawke and confident like Paul Keating and boring and self-interested like John Howard.

Scott Morrison, who holds office by one seat, tells the story of half the country. At the last election, that half of the country voted for a government with no agenda. This is a persistent myth that Australia tells itself: that the country is so comfortable it scarcely needs to be governed.

Morrison understands this well. It is the premise of his leadership. He exists to remind voters that anyone could do it, that so much is right with the country it could elect a glorified travel agent to its highest office and still get away with it.

When Scott Morrison says "How good is Australia?" he is really saying "Can you believe they put me in charge of this place?" This is meant as a form of reassurance: "If I can do this with no apparent aptitude or discipline or foresight, then surely the country is in great shape."

Of course, this has never been true. The past decade will be remembered as one of lost opportunities. It is with embarrassment that we will look back at the wilful ignorance of that position, of how much was overlooked to pretend we would all be okay.

The pandemic is not the beginning of this – it is the aftertaste of incompetence. The gross mishandling of every aspect of this catastrophe has a perfect mirror in decisions already made on climate change.

First experts were ignored. Then there was the appeal to exceptionalism. Then to the impossibility of doing anything ourselves. Opportunities were missed, especially on technology. Finally, the government decided to pretend it wasn't happening at all. When this became unsustainable, they hoped the market would fix the problem.

We are at the market end of coronavirus. Personal responsibility is the government's answer to its own staggering failure to take charge when it should have, when capacity could have been built in the public health system, when vaccines could have been acquired, when testing infrastructure could have been established.

Transport workers had been warning the prime minister's office of supply chain breakdowns since October. The issue was noted for mention in national cabinet documents leaked to this newspaper. Nothing was done.

There were early warnings on testing, too, just as there had been early offers on vaccine supply. All were ignored. The faith in the myth was too great: Morrison truly believed the country would continue to govern itself, as it always had done. He has a nostalgia for indifference.

Australia will for years pay the price for this certainty, especially on climate change. The next election will be a test of whether we have outgrown the myth of our own comfort, of whether we can finally accept that the country needs a person who can lead it, who tells a story that doesn't rhyme, one that is more complicated and aware than "How good is Australia?"

Hand-to-hand combat

Scott Morrison wears a lot of make-up. He understands cameras: not how they work but what they do. In front of the press he never stops moving. They are small moves, back and forth, to make sure everyone has the shot. He understands politics is obligation and opportunity and that his skill is the latter.

The American entertainer W.C. Fields refused to work with animals or children. Morrison prefers them above all else. He will spend half a morning signing his name on skateboards or bike helmets. He will read his daughter's poetry at official gatherings, stumbling along through the classroom syntax: "My land called Australia. My heart soiled in loving grace. My cherished home filled with love and ancient dreaming ..."

Morrison's is a politics of distraction, performed for a shallow media and a disconnected electorate. For the very reasons Fields warned against performing with children, he adores them. They pull focus.

When Morrison saw Grace Tame at The Lodge this week, he saw another photo opportunity. He has a tendency to mistake people for possibilities. He called her name twice before she walked over. "Grace," he said. "Hello Grace." The patter started before he shook her hand. He seemed surprised she wasn't smiling. "How are you going? Congratulations on the ... on the engagement."

The energy was familiar. Two years ago he tried to shake a firefighter's hand in front of cameras in Cobargo, New South Wales. The man refused. Morrison picked up his left hand and shook it instead. In the same burnt-out town he forced a pregnant woman to shake hands with him. "I'm only shaking your hand if you give more funding to our RFS," she said, her voice starting to break. "So many people have lost their homes ... We need more help."

Scott Morrison has said that when he touches a person he is laying hands on them. This work is spiritual. "I've been in evacuation centres where people thought I was just giving someone a hug and I was praying and putting my hands on people ... laying hands on them and praying in various situations," he says. "God has, I believe, been using us in those moments to be able to provide some relief and comfort and just some reassurance."

Morrison believes in the physical. As well as being religious he is tactile. His hands are bigger than you expect. His shake is dry and firm. It carries something a few beats short of sincerity, as if a handshake is an agreement and if he can get one he's done the deal. Morrison claims to be purely transactional and nowhere else is this more simple or more clear.

When Tame looked at Morrison and refused to smile, refused to mask, refused to play along, she was reminding him of something that should already have been obvious: if anyone has disrespected the office, it is him. Tame was not being impertinent but the opposite. She was showing Morrison what he fails to see is true.

Let me be me

The strategy, finally, was that of a school bully: find the most vulnerable child on the playground and make their life worse. This is where the religious freedom bill ended up, sweaty faced and shirt untucked, laying into a kid behind the bike sheds.

We don't know whose idea it was to make trans students the wedge on which Scott Morrison misbalanced his plan. Possibly it was Morrison's or Michaelia Cash's. Possibly it was a perverse staffer, unable to connect the reality of what they were doing with the political gain they were hoping to make.

We know that Morrison doesn't believe schools are a place for trans identities. He has said as much on radio. "It's not happening in the school I send my kids to," he says, "and that's one of the reasons I send them there." The line he reaches for means the opposite of what he pretends it does: "Let kids be kids."

Of course, if this were his intention he would not choose the most at-risk group of kids and make laws to specifically facilitate their punishment. He would not make their existence a question to be debated on the floor of parliament. When Morrison says "Let kids be kids" he means "Let me be me".

On gay conversion therapy, he says it's not his problem. "It's just not an issue for me and I'm not planning to get engaged in the issue."

When the marriage equality bill was voted for, he abstained. He lent no number to the rights of queer Australians. He said the ugly postal vote, brought on by the lack of decency within his own party, had affected Christians just as much. "They have also been subject to quite dreadful hate speech and bigotry as well. It is not confined to one side of this debate."

This last comparison, although false, is the premise of his bill to harm trans youth. He views it all as a trade: if you can get married, we need something else in return.

Everything to Morrison is transactional. He will keep dealing until the end, even if what he is left dealing in is the lives of children. He is Rumpelstiltskin, locked mad in a room, settling on a first born for his payment.

It's not clear how many votes there are in this. People of faith already live unimpeded. Inquiries have found as much. Many would see the bargaining for what it is: vicious and unbelievably cruel.

The bill has been amended, although not enough. Trans youth will be afforded the same meagre protections as queer children. This doesn't change what was intended: that their rights be offered up for the sake of a win. It is impossible to overstate how disgusting this is.

What Australia needs is not a crude piece of legislation to protect bigoted principals and doctors who want to insult their patients. We need a bill of rights to enshrine all principles of freedom. More than that, we need a government willing to offer one, rather than to trade on the edges with one life over another.

Cruel inventions

Perhaps there is a second world, almost identical to the one in which we live. It has the same brightness and dark, the same politics, the same families and friendships. Except for one thing: the people in this world wrongly believe transwomen are ruining sport. They believe that these women are taking quota seats on boards and that they somehow make bathrooms unsafe.

Scott Morrison lives in this second world. It is here that he sets about addressing imaginary problems, ignoring the ones that exist in the world where he was elected and the rest of us live. On Tuesday, he lent his tawdry support to a private member's bill from one of his senators. The bill would ensure the right of sporting clubs to discriminate against transwomen.

"I think it's a terrific bill and I've given her great encouragement," Morrison said. "Claire is a champion for women's sport and I think she's been right to raise these issues in the way that she has. Well done, Claire."

Claire Chandler could not name a single sporting group that had asked for her "Save Women's Sport" bill. This is because the issue is made up. It is an expression not of need but of viciousness. The political right has lost every major battle on equality and is now trying to invent a conflict with transwomen. As ever, they have found the most vulnerable group and decided to make their lives worse.

America and Britain are already into a pogrom against trans people. In Texas this week, the governor likened gender affirmation to child abuse. Last year, more than 100 bills were introduced to limit trans rights across the country.

British newspapers endlessly debate trans issues. A confused and fretful group has broken off from feminism, gathered around conspiracy theories and sly hypotheticals. At their most polite they say: of course transwomen should have rights; of course it is terrible they experience such high levels of violence and disadvantage; but we have to discriminate against them.

It is possible Morrison does not understand this issue. That would not make the issue particularly unique. Not understanding has been the defining part of his prime ministership – on climate change, on various emergencies, on the pandemic.

What he does understand, however, better than most, is division. He understands hate and its public uses. In the second world where he makes up policies, hate must function as a kind of life force.

In this second world of useless interventions, of problems he invents himself before pretending to fix them, the borders are ringed by refugees. Innocent men in hotel prisons are a threat to the public. Transwomen stand on the winners' podium at every sporting event.

Paul Keating once said leadership was about two things: imagination and courage. Every time Morrison attempts to exploit a panic against trans people, it is a reminder that he has none of either. He is small-minded and cowardly, just as Claire Chandler's bill is.

Capricious freedom

The message came from Mehdi Ali a day before the flight. The next evening he was going to be taken to the airport. He would be put on a plane and flown to America. After almost nine years, he would be free.

Even through the screen you could sense his excitement. There was also the fear that like everything else this wouldn't happen, that he couldn't celebrate, that it might be another cruel turn in a maze without an end.

"The same silence and the same terrible heaviness of everything is repeating itself. The cool air inside this cage is too heavy for our lungs," he wrote for this paper a few days before he sent that text. "I go to my room and sleep, and wake up in the same story that I have to live every day."

Ali came to Australia at the age of 15. He was a boy with a backpack, boarding a boat to flee oppression. He grew up in detention. "The law tells us that children must only be detained for the shortest period of time, yet I grew up in this cage," he wrote in January. "Justice is all I ask for. I don't want to survive anymore. I just want to live."

A few weeks later, he wrote: "I have read the Universal Declaration of Human Rights so much that I have almost memorised it. However, it seems that we are not part of human society and the provisions of the declaration do not apply to us."

Ali is a gifted writer. He knows how to make rain feel wet on the page. He knows that an idea can sometimes turn over on itself and with one more clause become the truth. To publish him has been an extraordinary privilege. To live in the country that imprisoned him is a source of eternal shame.

"People here are not only in prison – they are in prison with no charge, no trial, no sentence," Ali wrote last month. "We are here indefinitely. We are here indefinitely, to be humiliated by a system designed to crush our values, dignity and self-esteem. The worst kind of torture, in my opinion, is the kind that destroys a person's character. This – our character – is something we have to hold on to hard."

There was no reason for Ali's freedom, just as there was no reason for his imprisonment. The system is entirely capricious. This is part of its cruelty. People are trapped in a world without logic, a world of make-believe, built from a fantasy of safety that for decades has sustained the meanest parts of the electorate.

Both sides of politics participate in this. Neither is going to the election promising to free the men needlessly trapped in the Park Hotel. Nor do they make any offer to those in the purgatory of community detention. They know there are just enough votes in the torture of these souls to make it worthwhile.

"Unless the people of Australia stand up for us, we will not be released," Ali wrote a few weeks ago. "The government knows that. It is why we've been a secret to most of the public for so long. When an ordinary person with a good heart pays attention to our situation, they will surely feel our pain. Imagine how our family suffers? Imagine how we suffer?"

Grasshopper government

The original judgement was described as novel but only by lawyers. To anyone else it seemed self-evident that a minister should consider the wellbeing of children when making her decisions.

When the full bench of the Federal Court overturned the findings in *Minister for the Environment v Sharma* it was saying: the burning of the planet is not a problem for the government because the law is insufficiently clear on the subject of responsibility.

This is, of course, the view the Morrison government has held all along. Its ministers have never shown a capacity to govern in the interest of more than a select few. Still, to argue it in court seemed brazen.

In essence, the government was saying it could not be expected to consider the future. It would approve the extensions to the Vickery coalmine near Boggabri because it was operating only in the now. What happened after that was not its problem.

This is a grasshopper government, living on the edge of winter. It never got over the surprise of winning the last election. It never made plans. It never began the serious work of developing policy. It never imagined the future because it was still shocked by its fortune in the present.

It is hard to know what Sussan Ley felt when she saw the teenage litigants in this case crying on the steps of court. Possibly, she would have found it difficult to empathise with what the rest of us might call conviction. The might of government had been used to win a victory for itself and not the people it was supposed to represent.

In its judgement, the court was particularly worried about "indeterminate liability". It said there was a "lack of control over the harm". This meant that "the duty in tort should not be imposed".

But this is the point of climate change. It is why action is so important, because it is not one act that will answer the challenge, but many, taken at once, by each of the world's governments. The risk is so large that it will destroy the planet unless the planet is great enough to share responsibility.

After the decision the lead litigant in the case, Anjali Sharma, wrote: "Today's ruling does not change the minister's moral obligation to protect young people from climate change. It does not change the science. It does not put out the fires or drain the floodwaters."

All of this is true, but the Morrison government's view was formed well before the case went to court. That view is simple: we don't care.

Chicken suit politics

Every three years, whoever leads the Labor Party is stripped to the waist, covered in tar and feathers, and marched through *The Daily Telegraph*'s newsroom, clucking and scratching like a chicken. The ritual is designed to debase the leader and show Rupert Murdoch's dominance.

This time it produced a front page showing Anthony Albanese with his arms folded and the headline "I am not woke". The subhead read "Albo vows to swerve away from the Left".

The treatment was not entirely accurate. Albanese rarely vows. He doesn't swerve. He made modest commitments to respecting faith and engaging with business.

He practised his lines: "Labor's historic task is to move more people into the middle class, to appeal to small business, and if we don't do that, Labor won't be successful."

And: "You need to have successful businesses to have more workers working for those businesses. The key to both increasing profits and increasing wages is productivity."

He reminded the greedy that they can trust him. He owns three houses and will not tinker with negative gearing. He wants to spend more on defence. He won't govern with the Greens.

Asked if men could have babies, he said no. It was a bizarre question. It affects a few dozen trans men a year who choose to give birth. It was an odd gotcha, too, in that the paper asked it hoping he would get it right: of course men can have babies.

The interview was a reminder of how Murdoch's warped fetishes shape our politics. The agenda is set by men who will ask a potential prime minister "Captain Cook: Hero or zero?"

The answer doesn't matter except in a world where everything is part of an imagined culture war. This is a world in which a future prime minister cannot say anything decent or just without fear of approbation.

It has forced the opposition into three years of non-politics. Every thought is stretched over a fulcrum. Conviction is forgotten lest it upset the scale. "I was an avid supporter of marriage equality," Albanese told *The Daily Telegraph*, "but I also supported a conscience vote at the same time."

Recently, Nick Bryant profiled Albanese for *The Monthly*. The most revealing line came two days after the party released its less ambitious climate target. "Labor staffers seem delighted with how little controversy the new policy has stirred," Bryant wrote. "One points me towards Peter Hartcher's weekend column in *The Sydney Morning Herald*, which described Labor's policy menu not just as small target but 'no target', a phrase I thought might displease them but that evidently meets with approval."

This hollowness is the compromise Murdoch has produced in Australia. He wishes for a country as ugly and gnashing and spiteful as his tabloids. Sometimes he gets it. Mostly, he gets a country that looks like Albanese in his polo shirt: uncomfortable and uncertain and hoping to get by.

The ritual humiliation is over for now. The Murdoch papers will go back to scouring university pamphlets for evidence of the opposition leader's communist sympathies. Hopefully, if he wins, he will start governing for the country as it is and not as its clapped-out hacks wish it to be.

It's time

The remarkable fact about Anthony Albanese is that until about six years ago he never thought he would be prime minister. This may not seem surprising, but it marks him as different to his predecessors. Possibly, it makes him more normal.

He is not Tony Abbott, whose mother told family friends he would serve either as prime minister or be made pope. Nor is he Bill Shorten, who as a teenager announced to classmates that he would lead the country. Scott Morrison always made his rise to office look accidental, although confessed that God had visited him with signs and pushed him to run.

The fact Albanese does not feel preordained to office is important. It has made his campaigning tentative and uncertain, but it has also made him more diligent and thoughtful. There is no doubt that the platform on which he is running will produce a country more just and more caring than the one Morrison is promising. There is no doubt he would make a better prime minister.

"The thing about Anthony that I've always admired is that he's never forgot where he's come from," Morrison said in the final leaders' debate this week. "And he grew up in housing commission … and he's shown the ability to rise to be the leader of one of the oldest parties in this country."

And then: "But you know, to do this job you need to know your stuff. You need to be across the detail. You need to not make things up on the run. And you can't be loose on the economy … And as much as I respect what he's been able to achieve, I just don't believe that he's been able to demonstrate that he's able to get across the detail to do this job."

Tied up in this statement is a question Morrison wishes he could ask out loud: can you trust a poor person to run the country? He is not praising Albanese for never forgetting where he came from; he is reminding him that he shouldn't. He is saying: you have risen a long way, and that's enough.

Morrison is a student of class. He has borrowed its signifiers to exploit those less well off than himself. He knows how to pretend he isn't rich. He also knows that where Albanese comes from is someplace else, someplace where poverty means sickness and privation.

The unequal Australia Morrison keeps promising is a place where people like Anthony Albanese are less likely to become prime minister. They would be less likely to live in stable housing, less likely to have access to decent healthcare and education.

Albanese knows these experiences in a way Morrison cannot. When he says the country will always be fairer under Labor, he knows in detail what that means because he knows in detail its alternative.

In the final weeks of this campaign, it is becoming clear who Albanese is: a man who deserves to be prime minister because he never took for granted that he should be.

Life inside a lie

The government Scott Morrison leads has achieved less in three terms than perhaps any other in Australian history. What it has accomplished has largely made the country worse. It has dismantled an effective carbon price, antagonised China, cowed the national broadcaster, diminished the broadband network. It has confected a national circus on gay rights, alienated allies, rigged the tax system to ensure a country that will be less fair, where there will be less money for health and education.

Morrison's is a government of gross rorting and frivolous obsessions. It has no coherent plan. Its refusal to establish an integrity commission is an admission of just how bent its members are. It indulges peccadilloes on religious freedoms but refuses to legislate an emissions target. It muddled through the pandemic on luck and the work of the states.

Competence is a novel concept to Morrison. He does not possess it and nor does he expect it from his ministers. Billions of dollars are wasted on defence contracts. Billions more are rorted in election spending. It is government by boondoggle.

On refugees, he has refined a system of cruelty unmatched anywhere in the world. He will be remembered, if he is remembered at all, as the country's great torturer. He is a man who will not pass up even the smallest advantage. He is constantly chiselling at the nation's soul.

He has lied so often and with such certainty that the truth seems to slide off him. He is an oiled-up showman. In the early days of the government, when he was Immigration minister, he lied and said Reza Barati was killed outside the fence of a detention centre on Manus Island. The implication was that it was his fault for escaping. In reality, he was killed by guards. Morrison lied again and said social workers were coaching refugees to self-harm, and eventually his government had to pay compensation for this. It stands out as a lonely consequence in a career absent of them.

Morrison, this cruel and bilious man, now asks for a fourth term. He says he's just getting started. He plans to be different. He looks out at the carnage behind him, all of it the result of his ineffectiveness and ineptitude, and says he is a bulldozer. There is no crisis that doesn't begin and end with him imagining himself as a small boy playing with a toy truck.

His pitch, as ever, is comfort. He has the shape and bearing of a Jason recliner. He speaks to one half of Australia and promises he will make them comfortable. They will not have to worry about climate change or an unstable world. They will live in Morrison's Australia, protected by selfishness and indifference. They can live inside one of his lies, in a house they bought with their superannuation, safe in the constant present that is more accurately a suburban past. The future doesn't exist in this world because it is too real to consider.

Today, there is a chance Morrison will be re-elected. If it happens, it will be a tragedy for the country.

Anthony (2022–)

Mutually assured corruption

What is most curious about John Barilaro is the honesty of his politics. Not in the conventional sense of integrity or commitment to the people he represents, but in the way that the truth sometimes bubbles up out of him. Accused of pork-barrelling, he says: yes, of course, that's how we get elected. When given a trade posting, senior bureaucrats don't bother dressing it up: one tells the otherwise successful candidate her job offer has been rescinded because it is "a present" for someone else.

"There is absolutely no place for gifts of government jobs, whether they are statutory appointments or government sector appointments," New South Wales Premier Dominic Perrottet said after this was revealed. "Obviously yesterday the reports are concerning and from my perspective the independent review will look at that."

Of course, Perrottet is the liar here. Barilaro is a straightforward grifter. He knows what politics is. He knows his life has been built on the everyday venality of a system structured to reward ad infinitum every kind of seat-warming huckster. If the system resembles anything it is the milking shed of a factory farm, all sucking hydraulics and dead-eyed creatures caked in their own faeces.

The offer to Barilaro of a job in New York, greasing export deals and charging back dinners, was not an accident: it was how it works. Politics in this country is not a calling but a period to be endured in exchange for a pension and the chance of a plum job. There are exceptions, of course: too few to name here.

This rot goes all the way through. The last Labor government to hold power in NSW boasts more ministers in prison than it does ornaments to the cause. On both sides, at all levels, people walk straight from office into lobbying firms. The Morrison–Turnbull government produced more arms dealers than it did policies.

All of this is by agreement. It is mutually assured corruption. It started with meaning: once that was despoiled and besmirched, and enough people looked away in disgust, the Mr Creosotes of modern politics came for both parties. They fouled the preselection processes and poisoned the idea of talent. They made it so that by the time most people arrive in Canberra they are already grimy with the soot of the party machine.

It doesn't have to be like this. Still, it won't change while we pretend a back-scratching post in the Financial District is an aberration. It is the very expression of a system built to enrich the people craven enough to stomach it. In his own contemptible way, John Barilaro has made that clearer than perhaps it ever has been.

Scott of the autarchic

Towards the end of Tony Abbott's prime ministership, Malcolm Turnbull's staff began referring to Abbott's office as the "Führer's bunker". There was a general sense he had gone mad. He had fallen out of conversation with the public and was barricading himself in the suite.

At the time, Abbott seemed to be the worst prime minister in Australia's history. That was because Scott Morrison hadn't had a go yet. Abbott lied constantly. He was oafish and unimaginative. He used the office to prosecute petty vendettas and indulge antique fantasies.

Yet Morrison's time as prime minister made Abbott's look principled and even diligent. We now know that Morrison used the pandemic to build a shadow government of which he was the only member. He vested in himself extraordinary powers, giving himself ministerial fiat over Treasury, Home Affairs, Health, Finance and Resources.

"I understand the offence that some of my colleagues particularly have felt about this. I understand that and I have apologised to them," Morrison said this week.

"But equally, as prime minister, only I could really understand the weight of responsibility that was on my shoulders and on no one else. You are standing on the shore after the fact: I was steering the ship in the middle of the tempest."

Morrison's contempt for process is famous. He lives without contrition. He will say whatever he thinks he can get away with saying. It is strange that a man so fundamentally unserious could so seriously rig and bend the political system.

There is history to this. No one knows exactly why Morrison left tourism jobs in Australia and New Zealand. Inquiries found unusual breaks with procedure and a vast, grasping desire for power. What was unsuitable there became his modus operandi in government. Finally, he got away with it.

The question for Morrison always is, why? Why did he want to be prime minister when he had no ideas for what to do with the office? Why did he start amassing secret, unused powers? Why didn't he tell his colleagues? Why didn't he tell the public?

There is no real point in asking these questions. He is impervious to them. Every query slides off him in a slick of smirking and self-pity. He is a man without a why, an empty man inside of whom lives only the desire that makes true all the aphorisms about power.

You might as well ask why a monkey steals a nut, why a scorpion stings a frog. It is their nature. Morrison is confusing not because he is complex but the opposite. We cannot fathom how a man of his plodding inconsequence could have wielded such power and done nothing with it. The answer will never be satisfying, because there is not enough person in Morrison to make it satisfying. He just is.

When the Hurley burly's done

David Hurley didn't think twice. The nice men from Homes by Howe had done such a lovely job on the renovation he was happy to pose with them in photographs and appear in a promotional video. It was only later he realised what he had done.

"I made a mistake by agreeing, on the spur of a happy moment, to express my appreciation for the builder in a video and photos," the governor-general said. "I apologise for my mistake. I received no benefit of any kind for my participation. My words were not intended to be used in direct commercial advertising and reference to my appointment was not to be made. Nevertheless, I should have checked that my guidance was accurately followed."

Hurley is a glutton for endorsement. A few months after his renovations were finished, he began endorsing Scott Morrison's moves into various secret ministries. He didn't think to mention this at the time, either. His official diary records him presenting the Duke of Gloucester sash at the 2020 National Sheep Dog Trial Championships in Canberra but is silent on the fact that, a day earlier, he made Morrison Health minister.

Hurley says he was acting within the letter of the constitution. A spokesperson said he "had no reason to believe that appointments would not be communicated". Perhaps he should have checked, although it was a Sunday and he was busy at the anniversary of the consecration of St John's Anglican Church. This is the problem: the final oversight in the system is given to a person whose days are otherwise spent awarding ribbons to sponge cakes at district fairs.

Anthony Albanese has been at pains not to blame Hurley for Morrison's grotesque overreach. The solicitor-general found Morrison's actions "fundamentally undermined" both the principles of responsible government and the relationship between the ministry and public service. But, he said, the governor-general had "no discretion to refuse to accept the prime minister's advice in relation to such an appointment".

This might be so. As the advice notes, the rules around the disclosure of appointments are "deficient". It's more than that, however: the people with carriage of those rules are deficient, the system that places Hurley at the top of those rules is deficient, the very idea of a constitutional monarchy is deficient.

Morrison has moved through Australia's political system like barium sulphate. He has coated the oesophagus and stomach and intestine and showed up every fistula and imperfection. There is much to fix. Becoming a republic should be top of the list.

It is no longer acceptable for a vice-regal klutz to preside over the federal executive council or take responsibility for commissioning the prime minister. It is true that much of this is ceremonial but the experience of the Morrison era is that even ceremony requires oversight. Two men pretending to be competent can do a lot of damage.

Albanese supports a republic but won't offer one this term. He is right to prioritise a referendum on the Indigenous Voice to Parliament. But the government should not be afraid of referendums. There is too much wrong with the constitution, too much groaning history, to not push forward on changing it. Morrison is proof of that.

Brave cowards

Anthony Albanese was in the marginal seat of Gilmore, on the New South Wales South Coast, when he decided to reiterate his party's position on people who attempt to reach Australia by boat.

"The Labor Party's position is very clear – we support boat turnbacks," he said, halfway into an election he was winning. "And what's extraordinary here is that this is an example of the prime minister looking for divisions where there aren't any.

"The truth is that boat turnbacks have worked. The truth is that the Labor Party have been very clear about supporting boat turnbacks. I support it. Everyone in my team supports it. We'll implement it."

Labor's platform supports offshore detention as well. As deputy leader Richard Marles said the same week: "Let's be really clear. There is no difference between Labor and the government when it comes to border protection policy. Labor supports Operation Sovereign Borders and every aspect of it."

For three decades, Labor and the Coalition have taken turns developing the instruments with which Australia tortures refugees. The system is a tightly braided rope of cruelty and opportunism.

When Marles says "every aspect of it", he is being purposely indiscriminate. He is saying: even the deaths, even the immolations, even the emergency abortions, even the complaints of torture. There is no fraction in this system, only whole.

Marles has the politician's capacity to make the cowardly choice seem brave. This is the sophistry on which immigration detention rests, a trolley problem where the government both builds the tracks and then ties the people to them.

The just choice now would be to end offshore detention. Whatever processing the government pretends is under way could be done here. In a system built from lies they could just as well say it was a measure to save on costs.

It is unlikely this will happen, however. Based on form, the government will enter a contract with an American prisons operator to keep open the pretence of offshore processing. Millions more dollars will be wasted on a system that tortures the last few refugees being held on Nauru or shuffled through Papua New Guinea.

The moral cost of this is indeterminable. Little attention is drawn to it. The system is no longer about votes. The election passed without a panic over refugees, despite the Coalition's best attempts. Offshore detention persists out of habit: it is a just-in-case system, there because a generation of politicians convinced themselves it needed to be, and who now lack the imagination to see otherwise.

Perhaps the embarrassment is too great. To stop now would be to admit that the torture should never have begun at all. It would be like turning on the lights. And so instead these last few desperate people are kept in darkness, in conditions of unimaginable anguish, with no future in front of them and a past they have already run from, who down a shaky phone line say: "I am hopeless now."

Conferenceville

In 160 years of record keeping, it has never rained more in Sydney. With three months left before Christmas, readings have already exceeded the peak set 72 years ago. Parts of the city are inundated and buildings are set in the mould and decay of a third La Niña summer. Climate change is no longer a warning: it is washing away roads and growing in black patches on the walls.

In the same city, at the Conservative Political Action Conference last weekend, Ian Plimer said there was no evidence at all of human contributions to rising temperatures. Anthropogenic climate change was not real. "We are dealing with a fraud," he said. "A scientific fraud from day one."

Reasoning that his breath contained carbon dioxide, he said the test he needed to do was to kiss any woman in the room and not kill her. He did not promise – to use his favoured construction – that this would be colourless, odorless and tasteless. "Line up … outside," he said, "and we'll put this to an experiment."

Tony Abbott spoke at the same conference. Dominic Perrottet sent a video message, celebrating the people in the room as "part of a conservative movement that's driven by big ideas and bold action".

Teena McQueen, a vice-president of the Liberal Party, told those in attendance they should "rejoice" in the fact moderate Liberals had lost their seats at the May election. "People I've been trying to get rid of for a decade have gone," she said. "We need to renew with good conservative candidates."

These people would be the political fringe, except they have held the country's highest offices. The link between them and the flooded city outside is more than glib symbolism. The thinking in this room – if it can be called thinking – has been instrumental in holding back action on climate change and ensuring that whatever happens next will be catch-up.

When Alan Jones crawls on stage to say cutting emissions is like "signing an economic suicide note" he is repeating a lie that still shapes our politics. The timidity of Labor's policy is still guided by the imagined power of the people in this room, the wet-look quasi-academics and pocket-squared commentators whose influence is not influence at all but rather habit and narrow thinking.

Labor is persevering with the Coalition's sham carbon market when it should be introducing a carbon price. It will muddle through negotiating a safeguard mechanism when it would be more efficient and effective to simply tax emissions.

It is doing this because, even as the eastern seaboard floods again and a pandemic worsened by climate inaction spills into its third year, political wisdom says it cannot do more. This is the trick played by Abbott and Plimer and McQueen. The incredible thing is that the Liberals do not even have to be in power for them to play it again.

Don't look away

Emmett Till had three coffins. When his body arrived in Chicago, it was nailed into the first of these: a pine box, anonymous and utilitarian, indifferent to the significance of what it was carrying.

Till had been killed by racists in Mississippi in 1955. He was beaten and shot, his body tied to a fan from a cotton gin and thrown in the Tallahatchie River. He was 14 years old.

The men who killed Till believed he had whistled at a white woman, or flirted with her, or touched her arm. Decades later, the woman involved recanted some of her testimony. She said, "That part isn't true."

For his funeral, Till's mother chose an open casket. She wanted the world to see the crimes it had committed against her son. A photograph of his face, horribly disfigured, ran in *Jet* magazine, and then elsewhere.

The photograph changed how people saw the world. Likely it changed the course of the civil rights movement. The poet Claudia Rankine wrote that Mamie Till Mobley forced on America "a new kind of logic". She had insisted that "we look with her upon the dead".

In another picture, just as powerful, Mamie Till Mobley stands beside her son's coffin. She grips the timber ogee, the light catching on her keening face. There is a tissue in her hand. An unseen person leans into frame, helping to steady her grief. Inside the casket are pinned pictures of her smiling son, his eyes bright with youth, above a face that is now featureless and unrecognisable.

Two weeks after Till was murdered, an all-white jury deliberated for less than an hour before finding his killers not guilty. The state chose not to pursue the lesser charge of kidnapping. A year later, with the benefit of double jeopardy, the men who murdered him were paid by a magazine to recount the story of what they had done.

A third coffin was necessary after Till's body was exhumed in 2005, his family still hoping that new evidence might reopen his case. State law prevented them from burying him in the same casket and so the original was given to the Smithsonian.

This week, a 21-year-old man was charged with murder following the killing of Cassius Turvey in the suburbs of Perth.

The Noongar teenager was 15. It is alleged he was beaten with a pole as he walked home from school. After five days in hospital, he suffered two strokes, was placed in a coma, and died.

Again, his family gave permission for a photograph to be published. There is a tube taped in his nose and another in his mouth. His ears and skull are bound in gauze. He has the long eyelashes of a child.

There is little that can be said about this case, which is before the courts. What can be written is that occasionally an event will change the course of a country. Occasionally an image will so trouble the people looking at it – so appal them with its curdled familiarity, its stolen innocence, its senselessness – that it will bring with it Rankine's "new kind of logic".

Irrespective of what happens in court, the last picture of Cassius Turvey should do this. No country should be able to look at his unmoving face and not call into question all the structures and prejudices and privileges that went into his death. No country should accept that a boy could be killed walking home from school because of, as police have blandly speculated, "a case of being in the wrong place at the wrong time".

Angst into anger

In the headquarters of the Bob Brown Foundation is a sign that reads, "We're here to protect the forests, not our office furniture." Brown mentions this after he was arrested resisting logging in swift parrot habitat at Snow Hill this week.

"If they think we're going to be intimidated by legal threats, they've just misjudged these young people," he says. "There's a rising tide I haven't seen since the 1960s. Angst is turning into anger."

It is not clear whether Brown will be charged with trespass or if Tasmania's new, draconian anti-protest laws will be used against his foundation. "What they want us to do is stand uselessly on the side with placards while they drive their bulldozers into the forest ... They're trying to end the debate on the environment because they know they can't win it."

When the police came, Brown was waiting on a tree stump. Except for his height and narrow shoulders, he is exactly like the Lorax. The officers call him Robert. They tell him he isn't in parliament anymore. Two swift parrots fly overhead. At most there are 300 of them left in the world. As the police lead Brown out of the forest, loggers cut down the last tall nesting tree. It has no real worth to them: it will be woodchipped and sent to China.

"There's bloody-mindedness through all of this: 'We're not going to have greenies tell us what to do,'" Brown says. "It's unconscionable. There's no difference to the destruction of the Amazon. In fact, some of the bigger forests in Tasmania are more carbon dense."

If the Albanese government were serious about the environment, it would end all native logging tomorrow. There is nothing that justifies it. The industry could not survive without subsidies. It employs almost no one. It hastens the twin crises of extinction and climate change. The government is paying extraordinary sums to destroy the bush it is supposed to protect.

"A legislated crime is occurring here," Brown says. "There are parallels between what the government is doing to the swift parrot and what they did in the extinction of the Tasmanian tiger. They don't have a bounty out driving the swift parrot and other creatures to extinction. This time it's a consequence, last time it was deliberate, but the outcome is the same."

The world is in the midst of its sixth great extinction and we're letting it happen. Australia has led the contribution to that loss. In a speech to the National Press Club just after being made Environment minister, Tanya Plibersek made the same point. "We deserve to know that Australia has lost more mammal species to extinction than any other continent," she said. "We deserve to know that threatened communities have grown by 20 per cent in the past five years, with places literally burned into endangerment by catastrophic fires."

Yet when Plibersek visited Tasmania last week, she met with corporate miners before she met with environmentalists. Her government continues to support native logging. The extinctions she references are happening in the coupes where Brown was arrested. The laws in place to protect logging are really a licence to kill forests and the creatures that live in them.

"It's a very simple equation: if there's no nests, there's no birds," Brown says. "Their answer is 'We'll lock them up. We'll get rid of them. We'll frighten them off the scene.' Well, there's no way you can do that."

In 2002 an incoming Labour government ended native logging in New Zealand. The choice was an obvious one, backed by a petition and common sense. It would take very little for the Albanese government to do the same here, except courage.

Voice coaching

David Littleproud is parliament's leading aptronym. He does what his name says. Like a dentist called Stephanie Tooth or a plumber called Stephen Turd.

Littleproud voted against marriage equality. He promises to ensure the Nationals will oppose the central recommendation of the Uluru Statement from the Heart. He is intent on leaving behind even less than that with which he arrived.

"He's like a kindergarten kid, not a leader," Noel Pearson says. "The Nationals have foisted the mantle of leadership on a boy who's incapable of the leadership that's necessary for the country and for his party. I really think that the National Party is writing itself off for the future."

Pearson made a similar point when Malcolm Turnbull first described the Voice as a third chamber of parliament. That was a vicious lie to which Turnbull lent his modest political capital. It was likely the most shameful moment of his prime ministership.

"Malcolm Turnbull has certainly consigned himself, prematurely, to a footnote in Australian prime ministerial history," Pearson said then. "That is what he's done today: consigned himself to a footnote even before he's left the parliament."

The Nationals are running with the false notion. They say a Voice to Parliament divides the country down racial lines. Without waiting for detail, they say there's not enough detail. With only a fraction of the country's support, the party has forced back the prospects of a successful referendum.

"What every Australian should do, in the sanctity of their own home, is to make a decision about what's the best way to close the gap quicker," Littleproud says. "Let's not bring vitriol into this. Let's keep this sensible and respectful. Let every Australian get back to that core tenet."

Of course, the Nationals' early position has opened a window on misinformation. Pearson calls this the "tragic redneck celebrity vortex". Comment pieces have begun appearing in the Murdoch press. John Howard is reminding people there are few moral bars under which he can't walk in a top hat and lifts.

Peta Credlin, who was instrumental in destroying Australia's climate policy, is busy misrepresenting the Voice. She pretends it is a threat to constitutional recognition. In a foretaste of the lies the "No" campaign will tell, she describes it as a proposal for co-governance and invokes the spectre of a binding, quasi-judicial body.

"This is the fatal flaw in the voice proposal," she wrote this week. "It isn't the recognition on which everyone is broadly agreed. Instead, it's subjecting all the processes of government to a form of Indigenous vetting. The only way such a proposal could possibly pass at a referendum is through pretending it's less than it is; that it's really just a requirement that Indigenous people be consulted on the matters that affect them and nothing more. Even then, as we have seen, the plan is about telling voters as little as possible about what's proposed in the hope that goodwill alone gets it over the line and people don't wake up to the broader co-governance model that lies at the heart of the voice movement."

The Voice proposes no such thing. It is a threat only to paternalism and racist indifference. When the right cannot even be honest about what it is they are rejecting, it's because they already know how odious their motives are. That is the lie here: not in the proposal, but in the idea that its opponents are driven by anything but the most base attachment to the status quo.

Excited by competence

The night Anthony Albanese won, he told a room of supporters he would govern for Australia. For a moment he looked surprised. Emotion folded across his face. He buttoned his jacket.

"My Labor team will work every day to bring Australians together," he said. "And I will lead a government worthy of the people of Australia, a government as courageous and hardworking and caring as the Australian people are themselves."

These words do not seem like much. Character is the boilerplate of speechwriting. Scott Morrison's Australians were quiet and humble. John Howard's were comfortable and relaxed.

The difference is that Albanese was not projecting these traits; he was promising to match them. In Morrison and Howard's formulation, there was a subtle trick: these were not the characteristics of Australia, but the rules to which a person must subscribe if they were to belong.

"Tonight, the Australian people have voted for change," Albanese said. "I am humbled by this victory and I'm honoured to be given the opportunity to serve as the 31st prime minister of Australia."

Albanese was an unlikely prime minister, even to himself. A decade ago, no one close to him expected it. He was a numbers person. He did factional business. He was a capable deputy. His defining characteristics were his love of the Labor Party and his strategic cunning.

For the first few months of his prime ministership, it was not clear what this would mean. He had not imagined himself into the role and it was difficult for others to. Much of what was needed was repair.

Morrison had left the country in a scandalous state. His appearance at the royal commission this week confirmed what had long been plain: absent the slightest integrity or curiosity, grifting and obfuscating to the end, he was profoundly unfit to hold public office. The flag pin on his lapel, still there on Wednesday, as embarrassing as an unwanted gift to an exchange student, could comfortably top the pole on the parliament he led.

In his half-year of office, Albanese has easily bettered Morrison. The courage he promised has been there in his commitment to the Voice and his reforms to industrial relations. It has been absent in his climate policy, although there are signs Tanya Plibersek might use her portfolio to embolden Labor's ambition. His refugee policy is a disgrace.

After the worst government this country has known, it is too easy to be excited by competence. That should be a minimum. With Albanese, however, it is never clear that what he is delivering now is what he intends to deliver. He plays a long game. That works in state branches but not in response to calamities such as the ones we are facing.

"I firmly believe that Labor should be the natural party of government," Albanese told Karen Middleton during the election. "I believe that Labor represents the interests of the overwhelming majority of Australians at our best, and that we should be able to deliver that. And I'm determined to do that. Which is why I've spoken about two dates: this election and the next one."

Seven months in, Albanese has made an encouraging start. As a strategist, though, he cannot be left to believe he has two terms to deliver. The world is much too urgent.

Suburban black sites

In the detention centre at Villawood, in the west of Sydney, there are two concrete cells where asylum seekers are locked up alone. The guards call them "cool down rooms". In prison argot, these are dry cells. They have no toilet and no water. There is a single mattress and a closed-circuit camera.

Use of the cells is supposed to require approval from a detention superintendent. They are supposed to seek advice on the prisoner's mental and physical health. Time limits are to be strictly enforced.

This is not how it works. A report on torture from the Commonwealth Ombudsman says there is no policy governing use of the cells. There is no training, no consultation with health staff. The strict limits on how long a person can be kept like this are ignored. Records are almost non-existent.

At Villawood and elsewhere, mechanical restraints are routinely employed. Spit hoods are still in use. Intimidation and drug trade are rife. Women are especially vulnerable as there are not facilities enough to protect them.

On Christmas Island, guards sprayed detainees with fire extinguishers to control them. Footage exists of this but it was not mentioned in incident reports. On one occasion the extinguishers were discharged into a closed room where detainees were hiding. The ombudsman described this as a "pre-planned and systematic use of force".

In hotel detention the facilities were unclean and crowded. There was faeces in the bathrooms. Detainees were served food with maggots in it and staff decided not to replace the food because the maggots were "just on the vegetables".

Had this report been released while John Howard was prime minister, it would have been a national scandal. It would have filled broadsheets and led the evening news. Instead, it is met with numbness and fatigue.

The minister, having received the report, should have held a press conference and announced that he was closing the suburban black sites and island camps. Terrible things are being done, he should have said, and they will now stop. Instead, he did nothing.

Labor invented the idea of mandatory detention and is quietly sustaining its ugliest excesses. Last week it missed its deadline to implement the torture prevention bodies obliged by international conventions.

The voices of outrage are largely silent. The replacement of a despicable government with a less bad one has a calming effect. It makes no difference at all, however, to the innocent people being tortured in this system.

This is not quite the Overton window. It is not about what has been made acceptable. The average person would still object to isolation cells and maggoty food. The issue is something else: it is a kind of moral laziness, an indifference that comes from it being too hard, from the party of government being the one you might have voted in.

It is impossible to read the ombudsman's report and not feel disgust and sadness and roiling fury. The question now is what else does this government need to feel before it ends this unspeakable shame?

On Dutton

Say what you will about Peter Dutton, he is a terrible person. He is a man best known for his awfulness. When newspapers speak to his friends, most of them ask to be anonymous. The best they can say is he's funny.

This week Dutton's opposition attempted to restart a panic on boats. For all the talk of change, he springs back like a pig bristle. On Monday, the Albanese government finally granted stability to 19,000 refugees living on temporary visas. Most had been in this dreadful precarity for more than a decade. Almost immediately, the opposition was warning of another wave of boats.

"Now they have to send in the defence forces to try and protect our borders because the policy that they've implemented has put it at risk," shadow Home Affairs minister Karen Andrews said. "Now people smugglers will look at every opportunity to restart their trade."

Andrews was talking about the deployment of naval vessels to the country's north, weeks before the policy change. On Thursday, *The Australian* led with the story: "SOS to navy: get ready for boats surge".

It is as if the Liberal Party can never move past the thrill of the 2001 election, the one that put Dutton in office, the one that showed John Howard he could swing an entire campaign on a single lie.

For the Liberal Party, turnback is no longer just about boats. It's about clocks and progress. They are forever reprosecuting that one surprise victory. It's like a Civil War re-enactment, with Peter Dutton dressed up as himself and various frontbenchers playing dead in the grass.

The Murdoch press are happy to go along with it. They remember the Howard years fondly. It was a quaint time, when they had influence. Almost all the arguments of the era have been settled and almost all of them lost. Refusing to concede, they are now running them again from the top: on refugees, Indigenous sovereignty, climate change, the persecuted men of the church. Familiarity breeds contempt except where the contempt is what's familiar.

The cruellest part of John Howard's border regime was temporary protection visas. Research shows that the psychological damage done by these instruments of uncertainty was worse than the impacts of detention. They forced people to live in a no space. They were neither resident nor detainee. They could depend on nothing.

The granting of permanent visas to these people is cause for celebration. In refugee networks there have been tears of relief this week. For the first time, mothers and fathers can be certain where their children will grow up.

It is not surprising Dutton sees this as an opportunity. He knows there is a certain form of happiness that can be turned against the people feeling it. This is the happiness of the other, of people not like him. He knows that to the worst of Australia this happiness feels like a threat.

This is the real lesson of the 2001 election campaign: for fear to work, there has to be something at stake for both sides. Howard set up a struggle between one man's comfort and another man's freedom. There is a wretched imbalance in this struggle, which is why comfort always wins.

Dutton continues to claim he has learnt the lessons of the 2022 election. Until he can forget the lessons of the 2001 election, however, he will continue dragging the country backwards to its worst, most appalling impulses, to a fear of the vulnerable and a perverse desire to punish them for their vulnerability.

Canker-in-chief

The line has always been that Rupert Murdoch does not direct his editors. This is the pretence of his empire: that he doesn't need to direct his staff because they already think the way he thinks. The only problem with this is that it's not true.

The Murdoch who emerges from a 200-page motion for summary judgement filed in the United States this week is interventionalist and vindictive. He is filled with liver-spot cunning. He is opportunistic and unscrupulous. Democracy and truth are hostage to his extraordinary, implacable profit motive.

Murdoch, according to his own deposition, talks frequently with his chief executive about what is aired on Fox News: the topics of the day, which guests to have on. He routinely suggests stories. When he doesn't like what a host is saying, he will tell senior management to counsel them. Producers will intervene while the broadcast is still running. "I'm a journalist at heart," he says, without irony or heart or any sense of being a journalist. "I like to be involved in these things."

His son Lachlan is just as hands-on. He directs the network on content and guests and even where stories should be placed on the website. He texts notes on Trump coverage, directing programs in real time. He complains about the text crawling along the bottom of the screen: it is too hostile to his preferred candidate.

Lachlan Murdoch's directions are explicit. They are issued with full knowledge of how they will distort reality. He talks about narrative, believing he should control it: "News guys have to be careful how they cover this rally. So far some of the side comments are slightly anti, and they shouldn't be. The narrative should be this is a huge celebration of the president."

In the filing, part of a defamation case being brought by Dominion Voting Systems, Rupert Murdoch is openly concerned about alienating Trump or his base. "If he says 'Don't watch Fox News' maybe some don't." When Bill Sammon correctly called a Republican loss in Arizona, Murdoch personally made the decision to sack him: "Maybe best to let Bill go right away." This was intended as "a big message with Trump people".

Murdoch remains deeply invested in political outcomes. He presses his chief executive on the "importance of giving exposure to Republicans in close Senate races". He directed hosts to "say something supportive" about chosen candidates. There is no distance between him and the politicians who serve him. The pronouns blur into one ugly, suppurating, mutually assured mass: "We cannot lose the Senate if at all possible."

Murdoch's techniques have never been subtle but rarely have they been as explicit as this: "Just made sure Fox banging on about these issues. If the audience talks the theme will spread."

He knew his hosts were running a dangerous, fictive line when they claimed the 2020 election was a fraud. He did nothing. "I could have," he said. "But I didn't."

This case is about the interests of a private company, a voting system defamed by wild conspiracy theories, but it is really about the impact Murdoch has on society. He didn't care that his station was broadcasting a conspiracy theory. All he cared about was that it was good for business.

Murdoch is a canker on democracy, a man in complete knowledge of his influence and without the slightest regard to his responsibility. Everything to him is money. Sitting to give his deposition, he agreed with a phrase that will come to define him, the perfect description of what matters to him and what he will destroy to get it: "It is not red or blue, it is green."

Geppetto logic

There is something perverse about the prime minister announcing he will spend $368 billion to make Australia less safe – and for the press to record this as an act of political genius. It's like a child announcing he has fouled himself at the dinner table only for his parents to tell him how clever he is.

Standing on a dock in San Diego, squinting into the sunlight, Anthony Albanese removed from Australia's defence policy its last hint of free will. In announcing that we will buy old American submarines, he confirmed that Australia will join the United States in any future conflict. There is no way the boats would be offered if their use was not guaranteed.

The new submarines, which will follow these American boats, will cost so much that they will distort the priorities of the entire military. Worse than that, our own defence force won't really know how to use them. In all, their impact will be too meagre to act as a deterrence anyway.

News reports described Anthony Albanese as standing "shoulder to shoulder" with Joe Biden. This is an old fetish of Australian journalism: the excitement at seeing our politicians next to real ones from overseas. It's a kind of Geppetto logic and is the reason Scott Morrison conceived of the scheme in the first place.

In reality Albanese looked like a middle manager at an out-of-town trade show, checking for cut sandwiches because he'd spent his per diem sending drinks to someone else's table the night before. This is more or less the structure of the AUKUS deal.

The media coverage of this week's announcement has been foamy and uncritical. Essentially it is: defence spending is good, so more must be better. The groupthink is absolute. Both major parties see the arrangement as self-evidently right. China can only be a threat. Peter Dutton suggests we could harass the disabled to pay for it.

Even more galling is the fact that if the same spending were announced for climate action, the outlets celebrating Albanese's panache would be campaigning for his ouster. Over a similar period as the subs deal, we need to end our reliance on fossil fuels. We need to radically reform the economy and spend hugely to achieve transition. The project has all the elements of AUKUS, except it is actually necessary.

This is the real crisis for which Albanese should be preparing. This is the threat that will most impact our lives. Instead, the press and our politics are cheering a few old boats and some unlikely new ones and the chance to say America told us a secret.

Voice of a coward

Tony Abbott has now made his slithering, onion-skinned contribution to the "No" case for the Voice to Parliament. It is useful in as much as it synthesises the 12 key arguments against the Voice.

The first is that Indigenous leaders are asking for too much, that they want more than the symbolic recognition Abbott says a majority would be happy to grant them. "Let's be clear that it's no longer just constitutional recognition that many Indigenous leaders now want and that the government is proposing to give."

Abbott warns that First Nations people are really seeking a mechanism to address dispossession. He says this like it's a bad thing. He worries, as have others, at the country's decency: "the risk is that an abundance of goodwill might lead voters to support a change that turns out to be much more than they thought".

He says that, for Indigenous leaders, "the intention is to regain the sovereign power over the future direction of the country that they think was wrongly taken away two centuries ago". He repeats this construction several times. It hints at his long-held view: that colonisation happened a long time ago and that it was good.

This segues into his fourth argument: that history cannot be repaired. He notes that most Indigenous people have "dispossessing" ancestors – as if white heritage invalidates their concerns rather than expressing generations of assimilatory policy and violence. Borrowing from John Howard, Abbott says "none of us can be responsible for what happened more than a century ago".

His fifth argument is that a Voice would have input in all decisions, including of the public service. He describes this as "a form of co-governance" in which a small part of the population would have "a constitutionally guaranteed special and extra say over the governance of everyone". Looking at his career, it is no great surprise that he doesn't understand the meaning of the word "consultative".

He says the Voice is too great a change, that there is not enough detail, and that the government is rushing it. He argues that the Voice divides the country on racial lines and opens the way to High Court challenges.

He says activists would use the Voice to reinforce "different expectations about schooling, working and living". The body would "entrench the separatism that is the root of the dysfunction".

The overarching argument is that the Voice would be "a Trojan horse in the heart of our Constitution". This is a useful argument because its veracity is unknowable: if there were a hidden agenda, Abbott would want it defeated before it was revealed.

"I'd prefer to avoid the moral scorn that will be directed at all voice critics," Abbott writes. "But in the absence of an 11th-hour prime ministerial change of heart, it's absolutely necessary that Australia vote no."

There it is: the self-proclaimed prime minister for Indigenous affairs urging the country to vote "No". Underpinning all these arguments is his simple refusal to take responsibility for the past. Too much is at stake for him in accepting that colonisation damaged an entire people, that it was done by violence and legal fiction, that the foundations of contemporary Australia are bloody and inhuman and the impact of that amorality persists until today.

This is the one truth all 12 of Abbott's arguments circle: he and people like him will not accept any reform that asks them to confront their role in the ongoing dispossession of Indigenous Australians. Abbott's heroic self-image is based on this delusion: it is a cover for the poverty of his soul. The case for the Voice gets too close to asking that he and others confront it.

Plastic spiders

Peter Dutton knew before he called his colleagues to Canberra that he would oppose the Voice. The party room meeting was a stunt, like almost everything else in his career. Dutton is the ugly person who makes true the old joke about politics and show business.

There is nothing honest in Dutton's concerns about the Voice. His argument folds over on itself like a napkin: the Voice will be ineffectual and it will do too much. It doesn't matter that these positions are contradictory. His objection is not about logic. It is born of the simple fact that it is easier to throw a referendum than win an election. His success is the country's loss.

Dutton lives on the fringe. He talks about cities with scepticism and contempt. The real Australia is somewhere further inland. Presumably the men out there wear big hats and say what they think, if they speak at all. Dutton calls these "our seats". There are too few of them to win office but just enough to spoil progress.

In describing the Voice, Dutton continually refers to "city-based academics". He claims they would hijack decision-making. The dog whistle has peculiar harmonics: it suggests that education makes an Indigenous leader less Black and reprises the false division of "urban Aboriginals". The line also ignores the representative structure of the Voice: two members from each state, territory and the Torres Strait Islands; five more from remote communities; an additional member to represent Torres Strait Islanders on the mainland.

Of course, Dutton knows this but doesn't care. His cynicism is boundless. He pretends he is worried about dividing the country and finds that his only solution is to divide the country.

Dutton doesn't have the numbers – not yet – and so he pretends the numbers he does have count more. Steve from down the pub is more right because nobody asked him yet. This is how Dutton sustains his politics: he invents a miserable constituency and then pretends he is their champion.

Dutton is not a serious person. He doesn't have policies or eyebrows. His term in parliament has produced enough shame for six lifetimes, but this latest decision will grant him the balance for a seventh.

Noel Pearson describes him as an undertaker. He says he has betrayed the country. He says he will have to dig a very big hole to bury Uluru.

Hopefully Pearson is right. Hopefully the country is wise to Dutton's ghoul politics, to the creaking doors and plastic spiders of his rhetoric on the Voice. Hopefully it is plain to everyone that his small, fumbling objections are about only one thing: his hold on power in the cemetery of a once mighty party.

Poverty underline

In the report, the words of people on welfare are set in italics. The letters are thinned slightly and pushed off-centre, as if after being written down they are still straining to be heard.

One person tells the committee they rarely can afford meat or fruit and vegetables. They must choose between one of three medications to manage their pain: the others are too expensive and so they go without. "So, they're killing us, basically. They're not helping us. They're making us a hell of a lot worse."

Others talk about being made suicidal by the trap of poverty and the meagre payments that keep people within it. One says: "No one is choosing this."

The report from the interim economic inclusion advisory committee is clear and sensible. The million or so people on payments such as JobSeeker are being forced to live below the breadline. The government has one answer to this: increase the rates. The committee suggests it do so by 40 per cent.

"All indicators available to the committee show current rates of these payments are seriously inadequate, whether measured relative to the National Minimum Wage, in comparison with pensions, or against a range of income poverty measures," the report says. "People on these payments face the highest levels of financial stress in Australia."

The government released the report in time to avoid the evening news. Committee members were not briefed. The treasurer has essentially ruled out acting on its key recommendation: "The Albanese government will always look to provide support where we can to those most in need, where it is responsible and affordable to do so, and weighed up against other priorities and fiscal challenges."

Here is the lie: where it is responsible and affordable to do so. The greatest fear of a Labor government is to be big-spending. They have inherited a welfare system built on punishment and are too afraid to fix it.

Poverty does not help people out of poverty. The real costs are not in what is paid to the unemployed but in all the other costs that mount up on top of their alienation. In refusing to raise the rate of JobSeeker, the treasurer is condemning a million people to a life so difficult it is almost impossible to lift out of.

Over and over, the committee heard of untreated pain and skipped medical appointments. People who are too sick to work can't afford the medicines to get well enough to work. It is a cycle of privation, the constant lack and soreness of being poor.

The experience of this is foreign to almost anyone in parliament or the public service. No one who knew what $45 a day could buy would accept that it was enough. No one who had lived in poverty, the kind of poverty that separates a person and pushes them further and further from the rest of society, would suggest it was responsible not to help.

When Jim Chalmers talks about "other priorities" he should be explicit: is he talking about stage three tax cuts, or coverage from the Murdoch press, or something else?

Peta and the wolves

To Peta Credlin, there is little that separates Winston Churchill and Ben Roberts-Smith. Both made difficult decisions and lived with their consequences. To her, Roberts-Smith is a brave and rugged man, a soldier's soldier, "a hero, even if very possibly a flawed one, whose excesses, if any, are understandable in the cauldron of war".

Credlin, a former chief of staff to Tony Abbott, writes this in the newspaper Roberts-Smith used to intimidate witnesses. The soldier had a private investigator place a false story in *The Australian* about one of the people testifying against him. He had the same private investigator send threatening letters to another witness. Credlin does not mention this.

Instead, she writes: "And even if he were to be convicted of a war crime, to what extent, if any, should that detract from his undoubted heroics in winning the ultimate military accolade?"

She writes: "And if mistakes were made, at least some of the fault lies with us too; and with the senior commanders, now tut-tutting about the excesses of military culture."

Credlin repeats the central argument of Roberts-Smith's defence: that the men complaining about his conduct are jealous of his courage. She argues that a criminal court might find differently to a civil one. She pretends that the evidence was of heated decisions rather than calculated, ritualistic killing. "I'm not sure that any of us," she writes, "who have never been exposed to deadly combat, can fully grasp just how psychologically fraught and morally deadening this could be."

Credlin likens the treatment of Roberts-Smith to the treatment of George Pell and Bruce Lehrmann. She sees them as victims of moral indignation. It is no coincidence that *The Australian* has been a champion of all three men. The paper is a paranoid defender of privilege. It views all events through the lens of identity.

Not even war crimes can offend its fixed positions. The paper is untroubled by a court finding it true that Ben Roberts-Smith kicked an elderly shepherd off a cliff and then had him shot. It is untroubled by evidence he ordered another man be killed while he was being questioned. It doesn't care that he machine-gunned a

man to death and then took his prosthetic leg as a novelty
drinking vessel.

The Australian pretends it is taking a nuanced position, that it
has wrestled with complexity and is publishing what others won't.
This is nonsense. Its coverage of Ben Roberts-Smith is identical
to its coverage of climate change. It is contrarian to the point of
incoherence. It mistakes its agenda for doubt and treats this error
as a virtue.

Ben Roberts-Smith is not the victim of what Credlin calls
"the obloquy we seem so ready to confer on the pariah du jour".
He is the victim of nothing more than his own actions, actions that
killed innocent men, that diminished this country and the soldiers
who serve it. On the evidence that has been heard, he is a vain and
dangerous man whose capacity for violence thrills and titillates his
supporters, whose hubris has finally caught up with him.

Blue-suited chisellers

PwC has no regard for confidentiality. It has no regard for the public interest. Its desire to make money is aggressive and all-consuming. Its misuse of protected government information earned the consultancy $2.5 million, with the expectation of more.

"It is clear that the desire for personal gain trumped any obligations that PwC had to the Commonwealth of Australia and its citizens," a senate committee found this week. "This was a calculated breach of trust by PwC."

The finance and public administration references committee found PwC "supported and condoned" the misuse of government information by former partner Peter-John Collins. It stonewalled the tax office, misusing and misapplying legal privilege to hide thousands of documents. "It seems clear," the committee wrote, "that PwC's use of this tactic is not restricted to the Collins matter."

The committee notes PwC had a legal obligation to report Collins's actions but did not. It failed to make other disclosures that were also required by law.

"Taken together, the committee concludes that PwC engaged in a deliberate strategy over many years to cover up the breach of confidentiality and the plan by PwC personnel to monetise it."

The report goes on to say PwC has a history of cover-ups. It says the conflicts of interest inherent in PwC's operations were structural and dishonest in nature. It criticises the Tax Office and the Tax Practitioners Board for their slow and inadequate investigations. It says PwC is fundamentally conflicted. The company did not understand proper process and did not see the need for transparency or accountability.

"The question therefore arises: given the extent of the breach and subsequent cover-up now revealed on the public record, when is PwC going to come clean and begin to do the right thing?" the committee report asks.

"This leaves a further question unanswered: is PwC's internal culture so poor that its senior leadership does not recognise right from wrong, and lacks the capacity to act in an honest, open, and straightforward manner?"

It is rare for a senate committee to be so direct but it is rare also for a company to be so brazen and opportunistic. The culture sketched in the report's pages is ruthless and parasitic. The company is wantonly exploitative. Profit drives all. Ethics are nowhere.

This is the business, along with the rest of the Big Four, to which the proper functions of the public service have been outsourced. This gang of suckering management consultants have slowly taken over. To anyone watching, it is no surprise. Of course these Excel spivs are after only money. Of course their advice is rigged and loaded with every angle and edge of advantage.

There is an old joke about the management consultant who counts a farmer's sheep and tries to leave with his dog. The punchline is that he arrived uninvited and told a man something he already knew. The image is almost quaint against the reality.

Here is a group of people who would charge the government for advice and then on-sell secrets they stole in the process. It is a kind of double robbery from the blue-suited chisellers, a shameless assault on propriety.

Anthony Albanese has promised to end the government's dependence on consultants and rebuild the public service. On the strength of this report, it could not happen soon enough.

A poor excuse

At the end, robo-debt was about two things: a government totally unable to imagine the experiences of the poor and a politics that sees votes in their exploitation. Robo-debt would never have existed were it not for the contempt with which the political class views those living in poverty.

The word bludger is British in origin, but its full expression is uniquely Australian. Its root is in the word bludgeon, as in stick. It is still used in the same way, to beat and intimidate. The bludger is a standard of tabloid television. He is overweight and feckless. His life is too easy. He drinks in the morning. His children are everywhere and you are paying for them.

The royal commission heard that such a person does not exist. There is no man in a singlet ripping off the state. The evidence of fraud in the welfare system is tiny. The word the commissioner used was minuscule. She said this was not the impression given, however, by the ministers discussing it. They saw the grim advantage in propagating falsehood.

"Anti-welfare rhetoric is easy populism, useful for campaign purposes," Catherine Holmes found. "It is not recent, nor is it confined to one side of politics, as some of the quoted material in this report demonstrates. It may be that the evidence in this Royal Commission has gone some way to changing public perceptions. But largely, those attitudes are set by politicians, who need to abandon for good (in every sense) the narrative of taxpayer versus welfare recipient."

The commissioner noted the righteousness of rhetoric on welfare, the use of the word "cheats". She noted the conflations and the willingness to spin. Mistakes of fact were not corrected. Intimidation was a constant in public statements.

When Scott Morrison and Alan Tudge looked at the poor, they saw opportunity. They were Fagin-eyed and ruthless. The surplus they envisaged would be built from the manipulation of people least able to pay for it. They did not see this as upside down. They saw it as popular.

The media was part of robo-debt from the beginning. When the first stories broke about the flaws in it, the government used television and the Murdoch press to celebrate the toughness of the scheme. Private information was leaked to silence critics.

Journalists would approach the minister's office for any information that would keep the "welfare debt squad" on page one.

Some stories persist because they say something people wish were true. The welfare cheat serves several functions. He exists to remind ordinary, hardworking people of their virtue. He makes inequality a choice. He makes poverty a form of laziness. He keeps the battler at work because the battler doesn't want to become the creature he despises. Monotony is always better than sloth.

Robo-debt is a story of prejudice and opportunism. It is the story of how a government took broad intolerance towards the poor and turned it into political capital. The key figures will now have referrals made against them. Some may go to court. Compensation will be sought and likely paid.

Yet the greatest reform, the one that sits under everything, is the need to change how society values those living in poverty. The absence of empathy that sustained robo-debt, that aided in its cover-up, that excused its worst excesses, needs to be confronted not just in government and the public service but in the minds of ordinary people.

It is this indifference that made the scheme possible and that the country as a whole has a role in correcting. Poverty is not a choice and nor is it inevitable. It is an outcome decided by a society unwilling to make the contributions that would help avoid it. For some, this is hard to accept. It is much easier and more popular to picture a man in shorts and sunburn, a bludger, lunging at the camera that pretended to uncover him.

Class warfare

Julia Gillard (Unley High School) was at The Sydney Institute when she said the words that would help destroy the Australian education system: "no school will lose a dollar of funding". The institute is a confection of Gerard Henderson's (Xavier College), a shrine to hectoring and pedantry, where the world is held in harping stasis by a series of filing cabinets.

Gillard spoke before David Gonski (Sydney Grammar) had conducted his review of school funding. Her words ensured his scheme to address inequality in education could never be properly realised.

More than a decade on, funding to schools has never been so unequal. Government spending on private schools has grown at twice the rate of spending on public schools. In some states, funding has gone backwards. Billions of dollars in overfunding is being given to the schools that need it least.

Malcolm Turnbull (Sydney Grammar) helped this division. He capped federal government contributions, leaving public schools to slip further and further behind. He defends this, saying it stops the states from sneaking money out of the system. Scott Morrison (Sydney Boys High School) added his own perversity, topping up funding for Catholic schools and ensuring another wedge was forced into the system.

Almost every public school is now funded below the minimum set by Gonski. Almost every private school is funded above it. Teachers are leaving the public system, forced out by Dickensian conditions. In some places, where they can, students are following them.

Australia has one of the most segregated education systems in the developed world. The outcomes on literacy and numeracy are embarrassing, sitting at the bottom of global tables. All of this is by design. The numbers are right there on the funding charts.

Private education serves no purpose but to sustain inequality, to pass it on between generations. Parents pay to divide children and the state pays to help further this division. The promise at the end is networks and connections and more division. Nowhere else is taxpayer money used so lavishly or destructively.

When Gillard said no school would lose a dollar she was acknowledging a crooked truth of Australian politics: the unfair money given to the rich in private schools is sacrosanct. It is given without regard to logic or need. It is a kickback, paid to avoid charges of envy.

It is a lie to say private schools take pressure off the public system. In fact, it is the opposite. Private schools take money out of public classrooms. They entrench inequality. They create and maintain privilege.

The government is conducting a review intended to bring every student to the minimum funding level proposed by Gonski. Its target for this is the end of the decade. In the meantime, state school teachers pay for their own teaching materials. Classrooms fall into disrepair. Children are offered substandard education while others are treated as princelings.

The answer to this is simple but it would require the government to confront one of the persistent myths about Australia: that this is a classless society. The country's notion of fairness is confounded by one of the least fair education systems in the world. It is like this because it serves the interests of a small group of people in whose hands the majority of wealth lies. For others, it creates lifelong disadvantage. It divides the country in two.

Gonski laid out a solution more than a decade ago. It was hardly radical. He is a man known for his circumspection. Yet it cannot be implemented while governments pretend they cannot take money back from the richest schools and give just a little more to the poorest.

In defence of Marcia Langton

A key part of assimilation is the taking away of language. Culture is chased out word by word. This continues until a people no longer have a voice in which to speak, until they cannot tell their stories except in a new dialect washed clean of tense and history.

It is no coincidence that in the campaign against the Voice this is happening again. Forbidding words from usage is a powerful form of disenfranchisement. The rule now is that a "Yes" campaigner cannot say the "No" case is racist, even when it is.

If this rule is broken, they will be punished in newspapers and by politicians. Their judgement will be questioned. They will be blamed for losses being sought by the people doing the blaming. Their old speeches will be reread and taken out of context. They will be victims of the same upside-down thinking that lets the people holding the axes say the Voice is splitting the country.

Answering a question about the "No" case at the weekend, Marcia Langton told the truth. She is always telling the truth. "Every time the 'No' case raises one of their arguments, if you start pulling it apart, you get down to base racism," she said. "I'm sorry to say it but that's where it lands – or just sheer stupidity."

These are uncontroversial thoughts. If anything, stupidity is a generous out. The "No" case is built from racist tropes. It is Jim Crow cartoons and allusions to money and greed. It is caricatures of the angry black man, of the manipulative victim, of the "real" Indigenous Australian and the urban "elite".

For months now, the campaign for the Voice has been shown through a funhouse mirror. The people with the most power pretend they have the least. Clownish arguments leer up and take over. Infinitely more space has been given to Marcia Langton telling the truth than the "No" campaign lying over and over and over about what the Voice will do.

Langton was not judging "No" voters, although she would be within her rights to do so. She was warning against the specious arguments and base fears that propel the "No" campaign. For this she is now being punished. The idea is to hound her out of the debate.

It is not new. Alongside the taking of language, the colonial project was sustained by the making up of rules. These are the legal fictions that allowed a continent to be stolen and then forgave and excused the killings and violence that defended that theft. Their enforcement was lawless and inconsistent. The winners were always the same.

The "No" case runs on a knowledge as old as invasion: whatever you do, you will get away with it. Retaliation is the tool that makes this true. Revenge is the whip hand of power. The fact this remains the case is the very reason to vote "Yes".

Langton continued to tell the truth this week. It is a sad truth, one this referendum could hope to change. It is the truth of a fragile country, vulnerable to its own history and the ugly figures who wish to keep living within it.

"I think the 'No' case has caused severe damage to our social fabric and our democracy," Langton said. "And it will take a long time for Australians to recover from the viciousness of this campaign."

Toy soldiers

The word most used to describe Mike Pezzullo is "obsessive". He has the cunning of a stoat. He loves military history and regards himself a student of war. As a child, he imagined his toys fighting.

Pezzullo has a sour view of the world. His faith splits people into good and evil. He loathes scrutiny. Colleagues find him easy to dislike.

For a time, it was his habit to telephone politicians and upbraid them for criticising his department. At least once, his minister had to warn him about overstepping.

In other moments he would send senators strange, operatic notes: "How best to answer another's scorn? Answer according to the scorn, and one risks behaving like the other. Do not answer the scorn, and one risks allowing the other to be wise in their own eyes."

Leaked messages now show years of back channel intervention in politics. He craved laws to control the press. He desperately sought to keep immigration and security a portfolio of the right. He liked Peter Dutton and dreamt of Scott Morrison.

Pezzullo is obsessed with conflict but at the highest levels of his career he has made war only with refugees. He is an expression of one of the great lies of Australian politics, the one that mistakes brutality for competence.

While he was in charge, the worst excesses of Australia's immigration policy were committed. It was on his desk that the reports of child abuse and suicide were left unread. He dressed the public servants as soldiers and sent them out on the streets. He bent the language and defended the cruelty.

"There is no compassion in giving people false hope," he once said. "All that can be done is being done." For the people being tortured in island camps, he talked about "the quiet persuasion of those not owed protection to go home".

Pezzullo was in Kim Beazley's office when Labor proposed an armed coastguard. The idea of a Department of Home Affairs has been his for decades. He has spent longer than anyone building the poisonous edifice of border protection.

To read his text messages is to see the shape of his ambition. It is all gristle and transaction. He ran the ugliest part of Australia's bureaucracy without a second thought, just the hope that his advice would go to Dutton or Morrison or Angus Taylor or Alan Tudge.

It is unlikely Pezzullo will return to the public service. He has been stood aside pending an investigation into his conduct. His desk has been cleared out. Whatever war histories he might have had on his shelves have been put into boxes and taken home.

A reasonable person could hope that this is the end of a sorry chapter in Australian history, the militarisation of our borders by a man who never got to run Defence. Looking at it now, it is clear he never stopped lining up toy soldiers.

Labor has an opportunity for a fresh start, for a department that sees people seeking asylum not as enemies but as their first priority. We can only hope they take it.

Tight-shirted rage

The interesting part is the condemnation. Sky News describes the video as "disturbing". It says it was made by "a neo-Nazi group". *The Australian* calls it "racially charged" and a "Nazi horror". Peter Dutton denounced it as "quite horrific" and "unhinged".

In the video, a man stands in front of a burning drum. His face is hidden by a balaclava and his voice is twisted by a vocoder. "This is a message from the loyalists of the Warriors of the Convict Resistance," he says, "to the Australian government and Senator Lidia Thorpe."

The man makes a series of impotent threats and endorses "white Australia". He burns an Aboriginal flag and gives the Nazi salute. In an earlier video from the same group, the flag is again burnt. There is the same tight-shirted rage, the same backyard showmanship.

"Our forefathers did invade this land. In fact, they conquered it. The prize was the big red country and our enemy is the Aboriginal," one of the three men in that video says, continuing: "We will restake our claim as the rightful owners of this land, fuelled by the eternal and inevitable victory. When we burn the Aboriginal flag, we aim to offend the cultural sensitivities of the Aboriginals and their supporters, in order to make you feel the same pain and anger we feel when we see our flag being burnt."

For the right-wing press, the shock of these videos is the shock of a person hearing their voice on an answering machine. No one believes they sound like that. The lack of bone conduction boosts the upper frequencies.

Yet this is the argument of the "No" campaign, given a pair of black sunglasses and a hoodie and a spot under someone's fold-down clothesline. It is the argument of the perpetual victim. The language has the rococo din of internet message boards, but it is not so different to the case that has been made in the past few months: this land may have been taken, but that was in the past and it is settled now and we have nothing to say except that we won.

Some among the "No" camp argue the Voice will have unintended consequences. They claim it will forever change the Constitution, a document as fragile and unforgiving as tissue paper.

This offers an illusion of dignity. It says the "No" voter carries with him the wisdom of the law. He is defending a special, complicated part of the country, a sheaf of prudence on which we wrote down the binding truths about ourselves.

Of course, in reality he is defending only himself. He is defending a mean-spirited conception of Australia. When he argues, all he is arguing is that he is better than the people who lived here before him, whose country was taken. He is arguing that he won and he doesn't see the point of talking any further.

With the flames died down and his balaclava taken off, he is saying, as politely as he can: "Our forefathers did invade this land. In fact, they conquered it ... We will restake our claim as the rightful owners of this land, fuelled by the eternal and inevitable victory."

As outraged as anyone might claim to be, this is the message a "No" vote will carry. It is the message the "No" campaign has already licensed and driven across the country. The only difference is what it is wearing and that no referral will be made to the police.

The shrunken backyard

This big country is the wrong size. It has been shrunk over decades. The horizon has been pulled closer and closer. At some point the backyard became its largest unit of measurement.

The Voice referendum was an attempt to make it bigger. It was an antidote to the shrinking potion of modern politics. Its failure will work to keep Australia small and ungenerous.

John Howard knew all this. He is a reminder that not all brilliance is good. In his guileful, scheming way, he knew this referendum was about ambition. Its defeat would be the defeat of possibility.

Howard did not try to hide it. He has lost the patience for tact. "If this referendum is heavily defeated," he said, "which I hope it will be, that will discourage the current government from having a referendum on a republic."

It is not only the republic. Action on climate change is also less likely. Other reforms will be whittled down. Treaty and truth-telling will be driven off the agenda. Whatever courage the government may have had is now gone.

All along, that was the point. The "No" campaign was never really about constitutional recognition. The racism was sincere but it was never central. The colonial fantasies were indulged as a form of nostalgia but the real project was to collapse the foundations of the present.

Just as the history wars were fought as proxy, the referendum campaign borrowed one prejudice to express another. They were all worms in the same apple, chewing at the same mealy flesh. The enemy was always change.

The gloating and gnashing will last for some time, although not as long as the grief. Peter Dutton wants the prime minister to apologise for taking the country to a vote. He is drawing up sham inquiries, enjoying too much the humouring of his contempt.

In the days before the referendum, before the silence that followed it, Noel Pearson said the vote was about the generation to come. It was about the future. "My last pitch message is don't slam the door on the children," he said. "Imagine how horrible it is going to be that our children learn that the country turned its back on them."

On Saturday, that door was slammed. The dimensions of the country will remain the same, false and unbelievably mean. There is the same choking fence line, the same jealous lawn. There is the same sense of entitlement and smug, sour-tasting opportunism. None of this is fair or right, but for just enough people it is just enough. For everybody else, it is a tragedy.

Acknowledgements

First, thank you to Morry Schwartz, whose belief in *The Saturday Paper* has never wavered. Your contribution to journalism is greater than you know.

Thank you to all the writers and editors who have worked on the paper this past decade. You have made it something special.

Thank you to Rebecca Costello and the rest of Schwartz Media. You have helped make the paper possible.

Thank you to TV Moore and David Marr, who were there before it started. I borrowed from you both.

Thank you to Chris Feik for editing this collection and convincing me of what could be left out – and to Ziga Testen, whose design lends the book its wit and matches its silliness. Thank you to Urs Fischer for the image on the cover.

Thank you to Kate Jennings, whom I miss as much as I loved, who read a draft of the paper's first editorial and wrote: "Give me a reason to care. I cared. Once upon a time."

Finally, thank you to Evelyn Ida Morris. You remind me to never stop questioning.

Printed by BoD™in Norderstedt, Germany

9 781760 644901